CO-BER-062

John Arden

Twayne's English Authors Series

Sylvia E. Bowman, Editor

Indiana University

TEAS 378

JOHN ARDEN
(1930–   )
Photograph by Roger Mayne

John Arden

By Malcolm Page

Simon Fraser University

Twayne Publishers • Boston

John Arden
Malcolm Page

Copyright © 1984 by G. K. Hall & Company
All Rights Reserved
Published by Twayne Publishers
A Division of G. K. Hall & Company
70 Lincoln Street
Boston, Massachusetts 02111

Book Production by John Amburg

Book Design by Barbara Anderson

Printed on permanent/durable acid-free
paper and bound in the United States of
America.

Library of Congress Cataloging in Publication Data

Page, Malcolm.
  John Arden.

  (Twayne's English authors series ; TEAS 378)
  Bibliography: p. 161
  Includes index.
  1. Arden, John--Criticism and
interpretation. I. Title. II. Series.
PR6051.R3Z83   1984   822'.914   83-15377
ISBN 0-8057-6864-5

To Angela
—and the children

Contents

About the Author

Malcolm Page was born in York, England, in 1935, and educated at Bootham School. After service in the Friends' Ambulance Unit, he read English at Christ's College, Cambridge, took a diploma in social science at Barnett House, Oxford, and then followed four years' work in adult education in Hertfordshire. He went to Canada to take an M.A. at McMaster University, Hamilton, Ontario, and afterwards gained a Ph.D. at the Riverside campus of the University of California, where he held a Regents' Fellowship and wrote a thesis on commitment in modern British drama. In 1966 he took a post at Simon Fraser University, Burnaby, British Columbia, where he is now an Associate Professor of English. He has taught widely in drama, twentieth century literature, and Commonwealth Literature. He is married, with three sons and a daughter.

Dr. Page has published articles on such subjects as Arnold Wesker, Charles Wood, the Living Theater, British television drama, London's "alternative" theater, Canadian drama, Anthony Burgess, and West Indian fiction in such publications as *Modern Drama, Quarterly Journal of Speech, Twentieth Century Literature, Drama Survey, Journal of Popular Culture, Moderna Språk, Novel, Literature/Film Quarterly, Canadian Theatre Review, Commonwealth Newsletter, Journal of Beckett Studies,* and *West Coast Review.* He received a Canada Council award to research the history of Unity Theater, London, publishing his findings in *Theatre Quarterly.* His theater reviews have appeared in *Commentator, Plays and Players,* and *Toronto Theatre Review,* and he contributed numerous short essays to the encyclopaedias, *Contemporary Novelists* and *British Novelists since 1960.* He is Associate Editor of *Theatrefacts,* where his bibliographies of David Hare, Peter Shaffer, and Wole Soyinka were published, and is a member of the Editorial Boards of *Canadian Drama* and *Theatre History in Canada.* He served as President of the Association for Canadian Theater History, 1981–1983.

Preface

John Arden established an impressive reputation as a young man between 1957 and 1965. These were years of great excitement in the English theater, a time when such dramatists as John Osborne and Harold Pinter were first attracting attention. Arden first achieved recognition by winning a prize in a BBC radio competition. Then four of his plays were produced at the Royal Court Theater, London: *The Waters of Babylon* (1957), *Live Like Pigs* (1958), *Serjeant Musgrave's Dance* (1959), and *The Happy Haven* (1960). Three other major dramas followed: *The Workhouse Donkey* at Chichester Festival in 1963; *Armstrong's Last Goodnight* at Glasgow in 1964 and at Chichester and then at the National Theater, London, in the following year; and *Left-Handed Liberty* at the Mermaid Theater, London, in 1965. *Musgrave* was revived in London the same year and produced successfully in New York in 1966.

The first duty of the critic of Arden is to examine these plays. *Musgrave* has prompted more discussion than any other of his works, and its themes and import are still debated. *Musgrave* is also the play most often performed and most often studied. *The Workhouse Donkey* calls for some understanding of the English local government system, while *Armstrong,* set in the Scottish Border country about 1530, and *Left-Handed Liberty,* about King John and Magna Carta, need some historical background. All these plays show Arden's distinctive use of verse and song.

In 1965, then, Arden was an established and admired playwright. Most of the plays were critical successes and had been performed at leading theaters. Instead of going on to further acclaim since 1965, most of Arden's plays of the late sixties and the seventies appeared at more obscure locations and drew less praise.

While the plays of 1957–65 have some accepted place in British theatrical literature (if not in the British theater), the plays since then have not. Thus the critic's duty here is to draw attention to the considerable strengths of *The Hero Rises Up* (1968), about Horatio Nelson, *The Island of the Mighty* (1972), about King Arthur, and the hugely ambitious six-part *Non-Stop Connolly Show,* performed in 1975, about the Irish unionist and Socialist, James Connolly. Arden has also found radio well suited to his talents in such plays as *The Bagman* (1970) and *Pearl* (1978).

But it is not enough to praise the dramas of 1968–78. The critic must also attempt to account for the decline of interest in John Arden's work. I would suggest a number of reasons.

First, the question of fashion. Since 1965 such younger dramatists as Joe Orton, Edward Bond, Tom Stoppard, David Storey, and Simon Gray have attracted most attention. The issue is not merely new names. Critics for some reason find the complexity of *Musgrave* rich and stimulating; when they find similar complexity in *The Island of the Mighty* they consider it to be mere muddle. Second, Arden has deliberately rejected "careerism." He was dissatisfied with the impossibility of being involved in the actual production of his plays because, he wrote in 1977, the playwright "stands outside the working theatre to which he gives over his scripts complete for others to breathe life into"; he also "stands outside the general stream of non-theatrical society." [1] Arden found more rewarding experiences when more directly involved, taking part in the first production of his play for children, *The Royal Pardon,* at a community center in Devonshire in 1966, in creating a "war-carnival" at New York University in 1967, and in collaborating with a fringe political theater group on "Harold Muggins Is a Martyr" in 1968. He has worked with groups and communities in this way several times since. To write the *Connolly Show* was audacious as it played twenty-six hours on its one full performance, thus being obviously unsuitable for conventional theater.

Third, Arden's need to be more fully involved in productions led to well-publicized quarrels when *The Hero Rises Up* and *The Island of the Mighty* were presented, giving him a reputation for being "difficult." Fourth, his wife, Margaretta D'Arcy, has been credited as co-author of all the plays written since 1966 (except the radio pieces). Her contribution is difficult to determine and to evaluate, and she has been blamed—probably too much—for the fact that this later group of plays does not repeat precisely the strengths of such plays as *Musgrave*. Fifth, particularly since a long visit to India in 1970, Arden has taken more definite and extreme political positions, while still alternating between Marxism and open-mindedness. And sixth, Arden and D'Arcy moved in 1971 to a remote village in the west of Ireland, detaching themselves from the English literary scene.

Arden himself appears happier outside the mainstream of British professional theater. He wrote in 1977 that "I have been working consistently at plays and projects which have aroused audience-enthusiasm and involvement to a degree I could not have conceived fifteen years ago." [2] Tours of the polemical *Ballygombeen Bequest* in 1972 and of *Vandaleur's Folly* in 1978 have indeed taken his plays to new audiences. Arden and D'Arcy have chosen to be outsiders, both to please themselves and to maintain their integrity. Arden's writing since 1968 is not to be judged as that of one of the Royal Court group, but largely as work for presentation in particular contexts—though *Pearl* is significant by any standards.

This book is called *John Arden*. More correctly, it might be entitled "John Arden and Margaretta D'Arcy," as so many of the plays are collaborative. As it is not possible to isolate D'Arcy's contribution, in general I have merely stated when a work is jointly written, then commented in terms of Arden's styles and themes. Also, D'Arcy is proudly Irish and would object to appearing in an English Authors Series.

I have written of John Arden as playwright, including radio and television scripts, since, like most British dramatists, he has written occasionally for these media. Arden is also a poet, unpublished but for half a dozen pieces—though almost every play includes passages in various verse styles. He has published one short story, obscurely in Ireland, with a first novel announced. More important, he has written numerous articles, reviews, and letters to editors, a few of which, literary and political, are collected in his book, *To Present the Pretence*. Careful attention to all these would show Arden's changing ideas about the nature and aims of theater, as well as his response to such favorite writers as Bertolt Brecht, Ben Jonson, and Sean O'Casey.

This study begins with a brief biography. The chronological account of the plays which forms the bulk of the book presents summaries of plot, details of theater performances, and analysis. The account covers twenty-eight plays, framed by two unpublished radio texts, "The Life of Man" of 1956 and "Garland for a Hoar Head" of 1982. The final chapter attends especially to recurring character types and how they reveal some major themes of this remarkable playwright.

Malcolm Page

Simon Fraser University

Acknowledgments

My thanks are due to various colleagues and students with whom I have discussed Arden's work over fifteen years; I recall especially the witty insights of Virginia Cooke. David Copelin and K.E. Senanu corresponded helpfully about their own Arden studies. Arden himself kindly gave me a long interview; my wife struggled gallantly with issues of style. Thanks are due also to Simon Fraser University's President's Research Fund for a grant.

I was most grateful to the British Broadcasting Corporation for lending me copies of three scripts, "The Life of Man," a talk in a schools' series, and "Keep Those People Moving!" The British Theater Museum located for me the prompt copy of *Serjeant Musgrave's Dance*; the Mermaid Theater, London, allowed me to see the prompt copy of *Left-Handed Liberty*; and Motley Books let me see a copy of the unpublished "Harold Muggins Is a Martyr." The North-cott Theater, Exeter, kindly lent me the unpublished revised text of *Armstrong's Last Goodnight,* David Naden Associates showed for me their television film, "John Arden, Playwright," and Nick Hern at Eyre Methuen kept me informed of new publications by Arden. I was able to see the television version of *Musgrave* at the British Film Institute, where Paul Madden was very helpful. Part of chapter 5 first appeared in *Drama Survey.*

Acknowledgements are due also to Arden and his five publishers, Grove Press in the United States, and Penguin Books (for *Three Plays*), Pluto Press (for *The Non-Stop Connolly Show* and *The Little Gray Home in the West*), Cassell & Company (for *Ars Longa, Vita Brevis*, from *Eight Plays for Schools*), and Eyre Methuen, in Britain, for permission to quote from the works.

Chronology

1930   John Arden born on 26 October in Barnsley, Yorkshire.

1944–1949   Educated at Sedbergh, a public school in Yorkshire.

1949–1950   National Service as lance-corporal in Intelligence Corps; stationed in Edinburgh.

1950–1953   At King's College, Cambridge, studying architecture.

1953–1955   At Edinburgh College of Art, studying architecture. Students perform "All Fall Down."

1955–1957   Worked in an architect's office in London.

1956   "The Life of Man," radio play, broadcast.

1957   Performance of *The Waters of Babylon.* Married Margaretta D'Arcy: they have four sons.

1958   Performances of *Live Like Pigs* and *When Is a Door Not a Door?*

1959   Performance of *Serjeant Musgrave's Dance.* Moved from London to near Peter Tavy, Devon, then to Brent Knoll, near Bristol. Bristol University Fellow in Playwriting for one year from September.

1960   *Soldier, Soldier,* television play, transmitted. Performances of *The Happy Haven* and *The Business of Good Government.*

1961   *Wet Fish,* television play, transmitted. Moved in Spring to Full Sutton, Yorkshire.

1962   Moved in January to County Galway, Ireland.

1963   Performances of *The Workhouse Donkey* and *Ironhand.* Moved to Kirkbymoorside, Yorkshire.

1964   Performances of *Armstrong's Last Goodnight* and *Ars Longa, Vita Brevis.*

1956   Performance of *Left-Handed Liberty.*

1966   Performance of *The Royal Pardon* (Arden director and acting in it) and *Friday's Hiding.* Left Kirkbymoorside and began dividing his time between London and County Galway. Became Chairman of *Peace News,* resigning early 1970.

1967   February–June: Visiting Professor at New York University, creating a "Vietnam Carnival."

1968   Performances of "Harold Muggins Is a Martyr" (with Arden as Muggins), *Squire Jonathan,* and *The Hero Rises Up.*

1970   *The Bagman,* radio play, broadcast. Arden traveling in India.

1971   Settled in Corrandulla, County Galway, Ireland. Wrote, with D'Arcy and Roger Smith, "Two Hundred Years of Labor History," for Socialist Labor League rally.

1972   Performances of *The Ballygombeen Bequest* and *The Island of the Mighty.* "Keep Those People Moving!" for schools' radio broadcast.

1973   Spring: Arden and D'Arcy Visiting Professors at the University of California, Davis.

1975   Performance of *The Non-Stop Connolly Show.* Writer-in-Residence at University of New England, Armidale, Australia, in late Fall.

1976   Active in forming and shaping the Theater Writers' Union.

1977   *To Present the Pretence.*

1978   Performance of *Vandaleur's Folly. Pearl,* radio play, broadcast.

1979   "To Put It Frankly," 15-minute radio play, broadcast. Occasional book and theater reviewing in *New Statesman,* continuing 1980.

1980   "The Adventures of the Ingenious Gentleman Don Quixote de la Mancha," radio adaptation of novel, broadcast.

1982   "Garland for a Hoar Head," radio play, broadcast. *Silence among the Weapons,* first novel. "The Old Man Sleeps Alone," radio play, broadcast 22 October.

Chapter One
Contemporary British Theater and John Arden
Arden's Youth

John Arden was born in October, 1930, in Barnsley, York-shire, the son of a manager of a glassworks. He went to elementary school in Barnsley; to Terrington Hall, a prep-atory school; and then to Sedbergh, a public school in north-west Yorkshire, where he specialized in French, German, English, and History, and played Hamlet in modern dress. He says of Sedbergh School: "I personally think it is a very good one, with less nonsense about it than most of the Public Schools I've heard about. There was a good deal of sensible work in the arts." [1] Arden's education differs, therefore, from that of many of the other young dramatists of his gen-eration who came from working-class backgrounds and who left school at the age of fifteen or sixteen. Growing up in an industrial town in the 1930s, Arden was acutely conscious that he was "a member of the minority party in the class war."

Barnsley is an industrial town in the West Riding of York-shire, which is also the home of such other writers as Stan Barstow, John Braine, and David Storey; but Arden is not a "regional" writer in any narrow sense. Four of his plays are set in Northern towns similar to Barnsley: *Soldier, Soldier, Live Like Pigs, Serjeant Musgrave's Dance,* and *The Work-house Donkey.* The first two of these plays concentrate on the ordinary people of the North, and the two later ones on a broader social panorama. *Musgrave* particularly has a strong sense of how cold, harsh, and difficult life in the North can be. After Arden returned to Yorkshire to live in two villages in the eastern part of the county between 1961 and 1966, he

1

noted that the countryside there was conducive to an "historical or legendary" type of imagination.

Arden began reading Shakespeare at school at the age of nine and saw *Hamlet* when he was thirteen, but he attended very few plays: "As a small boy I imagined plays and actors to be circumstances connected with London—or at least Leeds—which were only visited as very special events." When he read George Bernard Shaw, it was only *Saint Joan* and *Caesar and Cleopatra,* while he understood Ibsen in terms of Shakespeare and Border ballads. He comments that in his late teens: "I found it hard to understand why modern plays needed to be written at all . . . I imagined the commonest costume of the actor to be that of a past period, and the usual business of the scene designer to be the reproduction of Gothic Castles or Roman Temples." This account of his schooldays' preferences prepares the reader for such plays as *Ironhand, Armstrong's Last Goodnight,* and *The Island of the Mighty.* Between the ages of fifteen and eighteen Arden began a few short stories and at least five plays. "I used to start one periodically, fill up a couple of exercise books, then it would get left," he says. These plays included a modern-dress account of Judas Iscariot, and one based on the death of Hitler was written in the style of T. S. Eliot's *Sweeney Agonistes.*

After leaving Sedbergh, he was conscripted for National Service; for, at this time, the universities usually admitted only the students who had completed their military service. Arden served as a lance-corporal in the Intelligence Corps. His time in the army was important for two reasons: first, he acquired a "private soldier's mentality" to counter the influences of home and school; and, second, after basic training, he was fortunate in being stationed in Edinburgh Castle and could go frequently to theaters. He admired the verse plays of T. S. Eliot and Christopher Fry, and his most exciting experience was Sir David Lindsay's *The Three Estates* at the 1949 Festival: "Underneath the colour and noise of [Tyrone] Guthrie's presentation I could discern the possibility of a modern drama that would deal as pertinently with the present ills of the world as Sir David Lindsay had dealt with those of the sixteenth century, and yet would not be compelled to renounce the excitement and splendour of the old theatre I had been brought up to believe in." Fifteen years later Arden used the figure of Lindsay in a drama of excitement and splendor dealing with the present ills of the world, *Armstrong's Last Goodnight.*

Arden entered King's College, Cambridge, in October, 1950, with an Exhibition (scholarship) in English, but he chose to study architecture. He commented: "To be a writer is a fairly chancy thing because there is no recognized period of training for it—you either are or you aren't, and you don't know at the age of eighteen . . . Architecture was a professional training which I found interesting in itself, and which I could drop if I found my writing developing."

Cambridge theater was flourishing at the time; John Barton and Peter Hall, subsequently the directors of the Royal Shakespeare Company, were then undergraduates. Arden failed an audition for the Amateur Dramatic Club, the leading student society, so did not act in Cambridge; and, as he was not studying English Literature, he had little contact with literary circles. Cambridge, however, gave him the chance to see many more plays; and he continued writing, completing a "tragedy on the Gunpowder Plot." He was "aware how difficult it was for new plays to obtain production . . . and such new plays as I saw depressed me very much."

In 1955, however, when he had returned to Edinburgh to the College of Art for the two years of additional training necessary to qualify as an architect, he was fortunate enough to have a play produced. This play "All Fall Down," performed by College students, was "a Victorian piece, about the building of a railway . . . very much in the style of John Whiting's *A Penny for a Song,* which came out at almost the same time." Arden now finds the play "rather embarrassing," and the manuscript remains with many others in a trunk in an attic of his Irish home.

Arden then worked for two years in an architect's office in London, living near Knightsbridge. When an interviewer asked him if his work as an architect influenced his plays, he replied:

It is difficult to say, except that it has made me very conscious of the stage designer's work in presenting a play. If you plan a building, someone gives you a schedule of accommodation. He wants two livingrooms, three bedrooms, kitchen, bathroom and so forth; you are given a site, then you have to put it together to ensure that it works on the inside, all the rooms open out of each other at the right place and at the same time it looks attractive on the outside. Planning a play is rather similar. You start, perhaps, with a story that divides itself naturally into half-a-dozen scenes (the rooms of the house) which you have to put together so that they work one from the other, and at the same time the thing has to add up to a complete whole.

The statement is vague, and, of course, Arden cannot say how he would view constructing a play if he had not had architectural training. The architect's office gave him the plot of his television play, *Wet Fish,* and in his work he traveled to unfamiliar parts of London, where he met people similar to those portrayed in *The Waters of Babylon.*

He continued writing, and his next play was "The Life of Man." This he sent to the British Broadcasting Corporation's North Regional radio, which transmitted it in 1956 and awarded it a prize for the best new play received. This award brought a letter from George Devine, who had just formed the English Stage Company, asking if Arden had any stage plays. Arden responded by writing a play about King Arthur which was rejected. Though he now finds this "extremely bookish and very literary," he used some of the ideas in *Musgrave* and later completely reworked it as *The Island of the Mighty.* His next play, *The Waters of Babylon,* which he wrote for *The Observer*'s competition for new plays, reached the short list in the competition, was accepted by the English Stage Company, and was given a single Sunday night "production without decor."

Arden as Established Playwright, 1958–70

Also in 1957 Arden wrote a television play, *Soldier, Soldier,* married Margaretta D'Arcy, an Irish actress, and, at the end of the year, gave up his job to become a full-time writer. He felt able to do so because the Company commissioned another play, gave him a part-time script-reading job, but paid him only ten shillings a script. His wife encouraged him to write full-time for the theater; and, when he inherited a legacy which, used economically, was sufficient to support him for a year, he devoted himself to writing.

In the first part of 1958 he completed *Live Like Pigs,* which the Royal Court presented in September only to receive an indifferent response from both the critics and the public. In the spring, when Arden accepted a commission to write a short play for the Central School of Drama, the only requirement was that there be eleven parts of approximately equal size; and *When Is a Door Not a Door?* was written very quickly. At this time, after Arden had decided to try writing in a remote country cottage rather than in London, he went first to Peter Tavy on the edge of Dartmoor and then to Brent Knoll, Somerset.

He stayed less than a year in Devon while writing *Serjeant Musgrave's Dance;* for, in the fall of 1959, he was appointed Fellow in Play-writing at Bristol University, a one-year fellowship. He was asked to write a play for performance in the spring of 1960 in the University's small, open-stage theater, and obliged with *The Happy Haven.* The play was later presented at the Royal Court, the fourth and last of his works to be played there; like the others, this one was poorly received. At Brent Knoll he noticed that the floor plan of the church was suited to drama; and, after he suggested to the vicar that he write a Christmas play, *The Business of Good Government* was first performed in the church in December, 1960.

Arden made his first public political gesture at the beginning of 1961, when he became a founder member of the Committee of 100, which was formed by Bertrand Russell and the Reverend Michael Scott to bring about British unilateral nuclear disarmament through civil disobedience. Other dramatists were members—Robert Bolt, Shelagh Delaney, John Osborne, and Arnold Wesker—as well as a number of performers and directors. Arden was not active, as he was not living in London; and, following his arrest and a fine for participating in a Trafalgar Square sit-down in September, 1961, he resigned from the Committee.

Arden's other political acts in the sixties included joining the Who Killed Kennedy Committee, which was formed to sponsor a lecture tour in Britain by Mark Lane. Arden's essay on the assassination controversy is reprinted in *To Present the Pretence.* In 1966 he became Chairman of *Peace News,* a weekly pacifist paper which covers the arts as well as current affairs, and served in this role for more than three years. Concerned about South Africa, he joined other dramatists in forbidding the staging of his plays there to segregated audiences; he also contributed the royalties from the London revival of *Musgrave* to Christian Action's work in South Africa. He was a sponsor of "Angry Arts Week" in London in June, 1967, a publicity effort against American Vietnamese policy, and in January, 1969, he took part in a sit-in at Rhodesia House, London, against Rhodesian racial policy.

In 1961 Arden scripted a half-hour movie, *Top Deck,* about a bus conductress in a suburb, which was filmed, directed by David Andrews. Another film script, about the Australian bandit, Ned Kelly, was commissioned by Karel Reisz the following year but was never produced. In February, 1962, Arden gave a Schools radio broadcast in a series called "Learning and Living," in which he encouraged his listeners to devise their own plays. He illustrated problems and possibilities with a playlet, "The Cowboy's Lament," based on the song "The Streets of Laredo."

Arden spent 1961 in the village of Full Sutton, near York, and 1962 in a cottage on an island in a lake in County Galway in the west of Ireland. The cottage, he comments, was difficult to reach and hard for him to leave. The only house on the island, it had no radio, television set, telephone, or newspaper, and he was able to concentrate on his writing. From 1963 to 1966 he lived on the edge of Kirkbymoorside, in North Yorkshire.

In the summer of 1963 Arden placed an advertisement in the theater magazine, *Encore,* which read: "Living as he does in Kirby Moorside [*sic*], a small Yorkshire country town . . . From which the Railway has been removed: in which there is neither theatre nor cinema . . . And where the population in general, deprived of their old social entertainments such as . . . A German Band, A Dancing Bear, An Annual Goose-Fair, The arrival of a daily Train at the Railway Station (all remembered with grave nostalgia by the older inhabitants) . . . JOHN ARDEN has conceived the idea of establishing a FREE PUBLIC ENTERTAINMENT in his house . . . It is hoped that in the course of it the forces of Anarchy, Excitement, and Expressive Energy latent in the most apparently sad persons shall be given release . . . Come to Kirby Moorside and help Arden to spend his money like water." [2]

Fifty people responded to this appeal, among them Liverpool poets, a fire-eating clown, and a potter who built himself a wheel and kiln. Shows were held nightly, and eighty people crowded into the Ardens' living room to see Charles Lewsen's *Bubonic Plague Show* and David Campton's *Little Brother, Little Sister.* Henry Livings and Jon Silkin performed; local people improvised scenes from unusual newspaper headlines; various films were shown and two were made. Arden devised an hour-long film survey of the town and wrote a commentary based on interviews. The month entertained many people, performers and residents, but Arden himself experienced what he called "a climate of fear" among so many strangers. Anarchy, he realized, was "a tightrope that can only be walked by a group of people all educated to keep their balance and not to flag in the middle." The venture is important because it demonstrates his concern to encourage community feeling where it is lacking or fragmentary, and in bringing varied stimuli to remote places.

After he had left the fun and chaos of this event, he participated in an equally funny and chaotic one, the Drama Conference at Edinburgh Festival. To the fastidious Harold Clurman, Arden at Edinburgh looked like "the traditional 'square' notion of what an artist looks like—long-haired, unshaven, unkempt and possibly illwashed." [3] Harold Hobson wrote more kindly that Arden resembled a "romantic minor prophet . . . as if he had come hotfoot from Sinai." [4] At the conference Arden argued for a Dionysian theater, a theme developed in his preface to *The Workhouse Donkey.* Early in 1964 Peter Brook produced the short play, *Ars Longa, Vita Brevis,* and Arden promoted in Dublin in the summer a revival of *The Happy Haven* in which his wife had a leading role. In March, 1965, a British Broadcasting Corporation television unit moved into Arden's house to make a *cinema verité* study of his daily life. In this film, which Arden thought to be "phoney and romantic," he appears not only as an intellectually alert, dedicated writer who loves the past but also as a rather harassed father who leads a hectic, overcrowded family life and escapes to lonely moorland walks. Two English premieres of plays were a few weeks apart in the summer, *Left-Handed Liberty* in London and *Armstrong's Last Goodnight* at Chichester Festival. At this time he also translated the spoken passages of Beethoven's opera *Fidelio* for Sadlers Wells Theater. Arden disliked his version when he saw a performance; the prose seemed "odd and wrong" in the middle of Beethoven; and he now thinks that the passages should be sung unaccompanied.

Early in 1965 Arden worked for a time on a television play about life in a middle-class suburb, a work which he never completed. In the same year he agreed to write a piece on war jointly with the Frenchman Roland Dubillard, the German Peter Weiss, and the American Paul Foster. The intention was that the authors would agree on five central characters and each write one act, but the project failed.[5] Two years later he began a free translation of Calderon's *Life Is a Dream.* When plans for a performance were abandoned, he ceased work. He also discussed writing a large-scale Passion play for performance in the Roundhouse by Center 42. In 1966 the Ardens left the Kirkbymoorside cottage, and with his sons now reaching school age, began to divide their time between a London house and the island in County Galway. Early September found them producing and acting in a new play. Again they chose to work in a small rural community, Beaford, Devon, with *The Royal Pardon,* a children's piece.

Arden visited the United States for the first time in June, 1965, when one of his plays, *Live Like Pigs,* at last reached New York, playing off Broadway. He made a second visit in the spring of 1966, for the premiere of *Serjeant Musgrave's Dance* in New York and also to take part in a symposium on "Alienation and Commitment" at Long Island University. When he returned in 1967 for a semester as Visiting Professor at New York University, he lectured on "Theater and Politics" in the small Humanities Department formed by Conor Cruise O'Brien, the Albert Schweitzer Professor.

He also led a weekly class for actors, writers, and directors in the Drama Department; and this group eventually staged an eleven-hour piece on Vietnam, coordinated by the

Ardens.[6] The framework for this extraordinary event was a Carnival, which erupted into a "Game" played out between rival armies and demonstrated how easily angry emotions are roused. Between battles, a play in twenty-four improvised scenes was staged, a fantasy allegory of American involvement in Southeast Asia. Arden here put into practice some of his theories on "Dionysian" theater!

In June, 1968, two plays opened in London three days apart: the political lampoon, "Harold Muggins Is a Martyr," with Arden and his wife in leading roles at the left-wing Unity Theater; the short play at the Ambiance Restaurant had a long title, *The True History of Squire Jonathan and his Unfortunate Treasure.* In the same month his new translation of Stravinsky's *Soldier's Tale*, which was praised as closer to the spirit of the original than previous ones, was first performed at the Bath Festival; it was televised on August 3. *The Hero Rises Up,* a drama about Nelson which had occupied him for several years, reached the Roundhouse for a few days in the fall. The next work was for radio, *The Bagman,* broadcast in March, 1970.

Arden, a Radical and an Outsider

When Arden and his family went to India in April, 1970, for a visit of several months, he was very ill for a time with hepatitis. He was invited to India by Satish Kumar, who wanted the Ardens to study the Sarvodaya movement as a possible example of successful nonviolent action and then to write a play about the life and work of Gandhi. The Ardens grew increasingly skeptical about the appropriateness ‘of nonviolence as a means to social change in India. They considered for a time a cycle of plays about such great revolutionaries as Jesus, Gaius Marius, Queen Lakshmi of Jhansi, William Longbeard, Toussaint L'Ouverture, Rosa Luxemburg and Gandhi; but the idea faded. In Assam the Arden family were imprisoned for a few days for lack of travel permits; the real offense was probably carrying Communist literature and planning to enter Nagaland, where the Indian army was fighting rebellious tribesmen.

India showed Arden Third-World poverty and suffering, as he records in his Preface to *Two Autobiographical Plays* and in interviews. In the Assam jail he found political prisoners who had been held three years without trial. He describes visiting a model steel factory near Calcutta and seeing nearby "pitchy creatures, naked and shining, staggering under slippery loads" in an oily swamp. Nonviolent means, he concluded, had failed in India; and he eventually approved of the Naxalites who selectively murdered landlords and money-lenders. This new attitude, which was to shape what he wrote, influenced the last of several rewrites of his epic about King Arthur and his times, *The Island of the Mighty*. When this work was staged at the end of 1972, the Ardens protested that the production was pro- rather than anti-imperialist.

After the Ardens had returned to County Galway, they were soon involved in Irish issues, for they bitterly opposed British rule in Northern Ireland. An eviction in their own village of Corrandulla focused their concern on the government's land policies, and they wrote the polemical *The Ballygombeen Bequest* about it, the first collaborative play of which apparently more than half was written by Margaretta D'Arcy. The play prompted a libel suit, which dragged on five years before being settled in December, 1977. The play was rewritten as *The Little Gray Home in the West*. Also in 1972 the Ardens wrote "Keep Those People Moving," a forty-minute Nativity play commissioned by schools radio.

When the Ardens spent the spring of 1973 at the Davis campus of the University of California as Regents' Lecturers, they intended to create and present a play about the years spent in the United States by James Connolly, the Irish unionist who was executed after the Easter Rising of 1916. They established a workshop, known as SLICK (Stage Left International Circus Collective); and they asked students for a commitment of six to eight hours a day, five to six days a week, for ten weeks. Problems soon developed; students resented the heavy requirements and mistrusted the implied politics; and the Ardens, who were shocked by the ignorance and complacency they found at Davis, wanted to raise political consciousness. Their attention shifted to local labor problems, particularly the un-unionized campus non-academic staff, while they also studied Connolly material in

the university library. Their workshop culminated in an
eight-hour show on the history of American labor: films,
songs, and improvised playlets about Henry Dubbs, the
archetypal "backward" worker, set in California in the
1970s.

Returning to Ireland, the Ardens continued writing about
James Connolly. Their six-part *Non-Stop Connolly Show* was
finally staged, directed by them with two others, in Liberty
Hall, Dublin, at Easter, 1975, the performance lasting
twenty-six hours. The Ardens also involved themselves in
community and political shows in their area through the
Galway Theatre Workshop from 1975 on. D'Arcy was the
leading partner here in a series of shows, performed indoors
and out in Galway, starting with "The Crown Strike Play" in
Eyre Square.[7] The next plays were presented in 1978, with
Pearl for radio and *Vandaleur's Folly* for a 7:84 Company
tour. Further radio work was a two-part adaptation of *Don
Quixote* and "Garland for a Hoar Head," about John
Skelton, while 1981 was devoted mainly to writing a first
novel.

Arden was appointed first Creative Writing Fellow at the
University of Leicester for 1975–76, which would have
given him the chance to return to England and perhaps
reestablish closer connections with mainstream theater. The
problems of *The Ballygombeen Bequest* court case,
however, forced him to decline the past at the last moment.
Late in 1975 he was able to serve as Writer-in-Residence at
the University of New England at Armidale, in Australia. In
the late seventies Arden and D'Arcy spoke at a number of
conferences and were prominent in forming and developing
the Theater Writers' Union. Arden also contributed a
number of book and theater reviews to the *New Statesman*
in 1979–80. The Ardens have thus been closely involved
with England, while continuing to live in a remote village in
the west of Ireland.

Nearly all Arden's most admired plays were written in the
eight years 1957–65, though he has written much since.
Now he appears such an outsider in the British theater as to
be nearly forgotten. The reasons are: that he lives in Ireland;
that the style of some plays is now even less accessible than

in earlier work; that his work since about 1968 has been
more explicitly political; that most of his writing is now
jointly with Margaretta D'Arcy, which perhaps changes the
nature of the plays, and that he now demands to be fully involved in productions of his work, often as director.

Chapter Two
Six Early Plays
"The Life of Man"

The radio drama, "The Life of Man," was first aired by the British Broadcasting Corporation's North of England service on April 16, 1956; a new production by Radio 3 was given in April and July, 1971. In this unpublished, ninety-minute play the action occurs in 1856, when a half-crazy sailor, Bones, is reliving for a girl his voyage on the sailing boat *The Life of Man.* Bones, who signed on as Second Mate on this "three-masted ship-rigged Liverpool packet, with a new steam engine set in her for no good reason," discovers that the policy toward the crew is "treat 'em dirty, sail the ship wet and dirty, feed 'em dirty, they take one arriving look at the Hudson River or the Mersey wharves or whatever, and there's none of them'll wait on their money to be rid and shot of this old *Life of Man.*" Bones finds that the other officers who are harsh and unfriendly are following the example of the captain, Jonas Anthract, who, tough and earnestly evangelical, tells his crew, "I'm going to make ye weep tears of blood, thereby fulfilling the commandments of the Lord."

The rest of the crew come on board drunk, the ship sets sail early on a Friday morning, and the superstitious sailors dislike starting a voyage on a Friday. When they pass a strange old women in a dinghy, she shouts a prophecy of disaster to them. Jones, a shepherd and a new member of the crew who was dragged on board unconscious, is "one of them black muzzled sheep-herders from the Welsh mountains," who is a kind of Pan figure to Captain Anthract: "It is a wonder these brown feet are not cleft / You have the appearance of a man / Would be all hair from the waist down." When Jones refuses to work and terrifies the others by whistling, which is thought unlucky, he is tied up in the rigging where

> I am beat about these Friday hours
> Cold as a churchless town
> Naked and dead as a black thorn
> Stripped and stark as empty towers
> On the windy ridges of the land.

When he is brought down unconscious and is appointed as assistant to the engineer, Captain Anthract still stubbornly refuses to use the engines; and the stormy winds drop after Jones has been taken below. Saturday is foggy and calm, and Jones lies unconscious all day "like a cracked-off yardarm, sort of straight and shining."

The remainder of the action occurs on Sunday morning when Captain Anthract abruptly dismisses Bones from his post for questioning the punishment of Jones and then preaches to the crew, "I have the Word shut fast in the storms and the waterspouts." At last he orders the engines started; and, when Jones comes on deck, Anthract, challenged, declaims "Who is the mightiest yet? Disorder, or the Word?" Then Jones speaks: "You have beaten me / You have broken me / Yet here am I . . . / I am the bloody bread / Strewn upon the tide."

The crew begins to dance and sing hysterically the chantey, "Whisky is the life of man," and the First Mate shoots three times. The engines stop, the ship is found to be on fire, a few moments later thunder rumbles, and the boat sinks. Bones, the only survivor, is convinced that Jones did not drown. He believes, too, that he saw a mermaid as he swam away from the wreck, and the play ends with the mermaid singing about Welshman Jones: "He stands up crowned with the golden rain / As tall as the tallest ship / And he leads them into a bitter dance / Where his death had been their hope."

Arden in the *Radio Times* pointed to two classical sources for his story: the so-called Homeric Hymn to Dionysus and the similar narrative near the end of Book 3 of Ovid's *Metamorphoses*. These describe how a handsome youth, with rich, dark hair, is seized by pirates, who find they are unable to tie him up; nevertheless, the captain will not release him. A strong wind blows, a vine and ivy grow, and wine flows through the ship. Then the youth, who is in fact Dionysus, turns himself into a lion and is joined by a bear. The terrified crew jump into the sea and are changed to dolphins, with one exception, the helmsman. Since Arden's character has Dai as his first name, he is also Davy Jones, the spirit of the sea, a kind of sailor's devil.

Most readers, however, will find the Christ parallels more apparent than the classical ones. Jones is kicked about roughly on Thursday evening; he is cruelly strung up until unconscious on Friday, when the sun is unseen all day; and he is then kept below deck until his startling reappearance shining on Sunday morning. When he gets the men singing during Anthract's sermon, he brings joy to the harsh male world. Neither Anthract's religion nor the First Mate's violence can cope with him, but Bones's good sense and humanity might if given the chance. Christ, and men like Him, would suffer as much if they returned to the nineteenth century as they did in the first—and so would Dionysus. Yet hope continues; Jones may have survived the shipwreck, Bones is compelled to continue telling the story, and it may be understood by some.

Two other influences are obvious. As in Samuel Coleridge's *Ancient Mariner,* a sailor is compelled to retell a horrifying voyage years later, a voyage that includes encountering calm and a gale, unexpected darkness, and an unfamiliar ''malevolent'' seaweed. As in Herman Melville's *Moby Dick,* a mad captain ignores advice, leading to a wreck with only one survivor. Arden has named two other sources, John Masefield's nautical novels, *The Bird of Dawning* and *Live and Kicking Ned;*[1] while yet another likely influence is Emlyn Williams's play, *The Wind of Heaven* (1945), which is about a Christ figure in the Welsh countryside in the nineteenth century.

Critics praise the work. Gillian Reynolds found it ''utterly spellbinding,'' for ''it sang of life and let the listener share in a rare glory of wrought words.''[2] Francis Dillon judged it ''an exhilarating radio play, radio of a quality we get very rarely these days. Where the story went by dialogue, the talk was taut and authentic; where it broke into verse, it flung itself into the magic winds."[3]

Arden establishes atmosphere with varied sound effects: sea and storm, songs and chanteys, foghorns, ships' bells and chiming clocks, a fiddle played in the room next to the girl's. The sailors' accents include Welsh, Scots, Irish, German, and Liverpudlian, while Bones seems to come from Hull, Yorkshire. Despite a title suggesting allegory, message is less important here than anywhere else in Arden's work; instead, what matters is plot, character, imaginative language, and a rich context compounded of superstition, cruelty, camaraderie, and adventure.

The Waters of Babylon

The Waters of Babylon, Arden's first play with a contemporary setting, is difficult to summarize as it is crammed with plot and invention, with ten major characters. Krank is the central figure, a Pole, a pimp and slum landlord in North London, and an architect, losing his job as the action unfolds. Paul, a Polish patriot, plans to kill the Russian leaders, Khrushchev and Bulganin, on their visit to England and demands the use of Krank's house to make the bomb. Krank refuses, so Paul asks for £500 instead. To raise this sum, Krank seeks the help of Butterthwaite, a shady Yorkshireman, who devises a local lottery, sponsored by Joe Caligula, an incorruptible West Indian councillor (elected local government representative). Krank meets Caligula at Speakers' Corner at Hyde Park, where he listens to Alexander Loap, a fatuous Conservative Member of Parliament, and Henry Ginger, a furtive, hysterically anti-foreign individual. Both men suspect Paul and Krank are plotting against the Russian visitors. Ginger decides to spy on them and Loap also asks his mistress, Teresa (previously Krank's mistress), to assist. Teresa proves to be the long-lost sister of Conor Cassidy, Krank's assistant in his various rackets. Caligula is enticed with an odd ritual chant by Bathsheba, a West Indian prostitute. A revelation follows: Ginger finds that Krank, who claimed to be a concentration-camp victim, was at Buchenwald in the German army.

The final scene is the draw for the winning lottery ticket. Krank and Butterthwaite plan that the successful ticket shall be theirs, but muddle the plan. Caligula sees at this point that his colleague in the lottery scheme is also the notorious slum landlord. Ginger has betrayed Paul's plot to the police, so Paul pursues him, but accidentally kills Krank instead. Krank dies, saying:

> So, only a few minutes to live,
> I must see can I not give
> Some clearer conclusion to this play
> To order your lives the neatest way. . . .
> Let the Bolshevik tyrants arrive:
> Conviviality shall thrive. . . .
> I'm going to declare my identity at last.[4] (96)

But he does not have time to give his identity—perhaps different from all those shown in the play—and finally Butterthwaite leads a four-part round, singing cheerfully, "We're all down in t'cellar-hoyle. . . . And we've nowt left but cinders."

The play was presented for one Sunday night in London in October, 1957, the fourth "production-without-decor" at the Royal Court. The object of these evenings was to show plays judged interesting, to find with minimum risk and expense whether they merited full production. Few critics described the performance; Kenneth Tynan attended and wrote: "Arden's piece (like certain novels by Miss Murdoch and Mr. Wain) is on the fringe of fantasy throughout; and when an author takes us into no-man's-land we are entitled to ask for signposts."[5] Krank was played by Robert Stephens, later a National Theater actor who portrayed Wiper in *The Workhouse Donkey* and Lindsay in *Armstrong's Last Goodnight.*

When *Babylon* was next performed at Arena Stage, Washington, D.C., in April, 1967, Julius Novick was as puzzled as Tynan: "It seemed that Mr. Arden must have had a point to make—nobody brings references to Buchenwald and Auschwitz into a play just for the fun of it—but what that point is I have not the faintest idea."[6] Robert Pasolli, however, gave an enthusiastic review, judging it "great

playwriting" because of "variety, imagination and
poeticism," yet also "a most unsatisfying play, as hard to enjoy as it is easy to admire." [7]

John Russell Taylor, the critic, attributes audience uncertainty at Arden's plays to his failure to judge; "you never
know where he stands." [8] The problem here is Krank, a complex figure, corrupt, yet amiable and well liked. As Arden
told me, "Krank is sympathized with as a charming person,
but there's no sympathy with what he's doing. You can be
anti-social and con people, and still be nice. After all, the
charming rogue is a very old convention." A light touch
prevents spectators from taking Krank too seriously, as with
Christopher Isherwood's Mr. Norris. Krank practices self-
interest in an amoral world, perhaps because of his wartime
experiences. He partly explains himself in a long speech:

> But I don't know what *you* are.
> Or you, Henry Ginger, or all of the rest of you,
> With your pistols and your orations,
> And your bombs in my private house,
> And your fury, and your national pride and honour.
> This is the lunacy,
> This was the cause, the carrying through
> Of all the insensate war
> This is the rage and purposed madness of your lives,
> That *I*, Krank, do not know. I *will* not know it,
> Because, if I know it, from that tight day forward,
> I am a man of time, place, society, and accident:
> Which is what I must not be. Do you understand me?
> The world is running mad in every direction.
> It is quicksilver, shattered, here, here, here, here,
> All over the floor. Go on, hurtle after it,
> Chase it, dear Paul. But I choose to follow
> Only such fragments as I can easily catch,
> I catch them, I keep them such time as I choose,
> Then roll them away down and follow another.
> Is that philosophy? It is a reason, anyway,
> Why I am content to hold such a disgusting lodging-house. (81)

Krank, in short, wants to be a free man, to be inner-directed
in a world he judges mad and corrupt. The speech suggests,
too, that this is a play of fragments, with first one chased,

and then another. The world is shattered and one should not hope to make total sense of it.

Krank's downfall comes when he is forced into a more public existence, associating with Butterthwaite and Caligula to raise money quickly. One of the most comic scenes is his effort to remain the businesslike architect when harassed by the sudden reappearance of both Teresa and Paul. This theme, the obligations of public life, recurs in *The Workhouse Donkey* and *Armstrong's Last Goodnight*. The portrait of Krank touches on the question of identity: he is an architect's assistant from 9:30 till 5:30 daily, he is slum landlord and pimp, he is called Cash in his dealings with Caligula—and he may also be the crank his name suggests. Conventional judgments are challenged: pimps and prostitutes are likable; architects, Polish exiles, Members of Parliament may be disreputable.

Arden describes *Babylon* as "an old-fashioned low-life comedy" about "the complex international life of Notting Hill" (in North London), adding "I had just come from the provinces when I wrote it and was fascinated by London life. It is the play of a young man coming to London." [9] His new-Mayhew view includes slums, Baker Street Underground station, Speakers' Corner, and a flag-bedecked town hall. The title points to the theme of exile. Seven characters are not native Londoners: two are Poles, two West Indians, two Irish, and one is from Yorkshire. London, a modern Babylon, corrupts them in every case.

This play was the first to show black immigrants to Britain. Arden is prescient in treating the race problem a year before it became a big social issue, with England's first race riots—in Notting Hill. As in Brendan Behan's *The Hostage* (1958), the serious and topical subjects—Khruschev's visit to Britain (which occurred in April, 1956), prostitution, slum landlords, the morality of Premium Bonds—are treated lightly. Unlike later plays, Arden finds it unimportant to be earnest about such issues. Some episodes are satiric, on patriotism, free speech, sexual hypocrisy, local and national government.

Essentially, *Babylon* is a wild, boisterous romp, like Behan's *The Hostage* and Bernard Kop's *The Hamlet of*

Stepney Green (1958), both of which it precedes. Arden
seizes a crowd of unusual characters—and some familiar
ones, like a pompous M.P.—and sets them off, interacting
energetically, with songs, verse, and poetic passages, as in
the plays of Behan and Kops. Arden's Irish characters rival
the eloquence of John Synge or Sean O'Casey; Cassidy says
of some girls: "No sea-weed but all roaring gorse, wild
white-thorn, a chiming tempest of girls, turned that dirty
Euston into a true windswept altitude, a crystal mountain-
top for love" (42).

The enjoyment is of language *and* parody of stage Irishness; parody is dominant in the Hyde Park Corner speeches.
Verse sections comment allusively on leading ideas; Krank's
"To look for true love in a naked bed / It is more dangerous,
perhaps more vain, / Than burgling a house on fire" (36)
reveals something of his foolhardy attitudes, and his "I
stood in the street / With the rain upon my feet; / While my
house so majestical / Did fall" (41) warns that he will eventually fail. Looking back, however, Arden believes many
scenes would be improved by his using a more natural
prose.[10] The use of song is one of several Brechtian influences in the play: the audience is directly addressed; its
sympathy is not sought; the approach to almost all characters is tolerant and understanding. Simon Trussler has, in
fact, placed the play as "probably the first entirely Brechtian
play in the language."[11]

Arden mentions several sources for the play. A rather
mysterious Pole resembling Krank once worked in an adjoin-
ing architect's office, and a friend suggested that he might
make a subject for a play. "I was trying to find what made
him do what he did,"[12] says Arden. At Hyde Park Corner, he
saw the original of Henry Ginger, speaking as he does in the
play, and a black who might well have been a councillor talking of Notting Hill housing. Arden also wanted to comment
satirically on the Premium Bonds scheme, introduced in the
Fall of 1956 and much criticized as the first State encourage-
ment of gambling.

He had two Elizabethan plays in mind, Ben Jonson's *The
Alchemist* and George Chapman's *The Blind Beggar of Alex-
andria.*[13] The beggar, an Arabian Night's figure, has several

identities, like Krank, and Face in *The Alchemist* disguises himself. Chapman's text is fragmentary, and Arden often finds this stimulating. These older plays balance entertainment with challenges to conventional morality and create unease about materialistic values.

Arden's interest in Krank continued, and he appears again in *Wet Fish,* while Butterthwaite's earlier career is traced in *The Workhouse Donkey.* Arden describes these two plays, *Babylon* and *Soldier, Soldier* as "a sort of North Country tetraology. . . . I've just, slightly inconsistently, mixed the same characters through four plays." [14]

Live Like Pigs

Live Like Pigs resembles *Babylon* in episodic form with numerous characters. The scene is a housing estate in a Northern industrial town (because public housing is so widespread in Britain, less stigma is attached to it than in America). The Sawney menage are rehoused after eviction from a derelict tramcar. They are wanderers, who live by making and selling clothes pegs, occasional work, and petty theft. They are, Arden explains, "an anachronism . . . descendants of the 'sturdy beggars' of the sixteenth century . . . today . . . there are too many buildings in Britain, and there is just no room for nomads" (101).[15]

Sailor Sawney, a tough old drunkard, lives with Big Rachel, "a tall handsome termagant," Rosie, a tired, sullen woman who has two children, Sally and a baby, and the loutish teen-ager Col, with "swift and violent mannerisms." The family resent being forced into a house; being unaccustomed to renting, they do not know whether or not the house belongs to them. From the start they live like pigs, neglecting the house and snubbing the well-meaning Housing Department official and the doctor. Three vagrant acquaintances of the Sawneys move in on them: Blackmouth, half-gypsy, the father of Rosie's children and now an escaped convict; Old Croaker, "a batty old hag, alternately skittish and comatose," who spends most of her time tearing up paper; and her strange, sick daughter, Daffodil, with "an old, old face like that of a malicious fairy" (103). The Sawneys are scared of all three, and relieved when Black-

mouth leaves, after a fight with Col about Daffodil, though
Blackmouth stays near the house for a time, howling, apparently mad. Next door live a dull, conventional family, the
Jacksons, whom Arden describes as "undistinguished but not
contemptible." Relations between the Sawneys and the Jacksons are soon hostile. Mrs. Jackson resents their rudeness and
noise from the start, while Mr. Jackson sleeps with Rachel,
then is angered by her. Col assaults Doreen, the Jacksons'
daughter—though she has encouraged him—and Old
Croaker steals and tears up their washing. The Sawneys are
suspected of killing the Jacksons' cat.

Feeling in the district rises, and Col is attacked. A mob
besieges the house; police disperse the crowd, then plan to
evict the household. Sailor is injured by a policeman and
believes he is dying, as Col and Daffodil run away, followed
by Rachel. At the play's conclusion Sally and Old Croaker
chant a spell that they pathetically hope will protect them, a
kind of protest against a rational and ordered world: "Mary
and Jesus and the Twelve Tall Riders / Nobody else nobody
else nick nack noo (189).

George Devine and Anthony Page directed the play at the
Royal Court Theater on September 30, 1958, for a run of
only twenty-three performances. The case was distinguished.
The part of Rachel was written with Anna Manahan in mind.
Arden's wife acted Rosie, Wilfred Lawson played Sailor, and
Robert Shaw, Blackmouth. Alan Dobie—seen the following
year as Hurst in *Musgrave*—was Col, and Frances Cuka, best-
known as the original Jo in Shelagh Delaney's *A Taste of
Honey*, was Daffodil.

In 1965 *Pigs* was performed by Glasgow Citizens' Theater
and by Boston Theater Company, who gave an off-
Broadway run of 128 performances. Théâtre Est de Paris
produced *Pigs* in 1966 in an industrial suburb, where the
audience related it to the Algerians who live in shantytowns
outside the city. The drama was successfully revived at the
Theater Upstairs in London on February 4, 1972.

Critical response varied. Laurence Kitchin wrote: "Arden
off form can be very bad indeed. *Live Like Pigs* . . . is like a
parody of Theatre in the Raw, awash with rugged
exoticism." [16] T.C. Worsley thought it "sprawling and too

crowded with irrelevant detail," [17] and Richard Gilman found "it suffers from a central opacity and its dramatic trajectory is impeded." [18] Henry Hewes of the *Saturday Review,* on the other hand, saw "a piece for actors to fill with their vitality." [19] Robert Hatch is an admirer: "A boisterous, driving outburst of human spirit under compression, it plays like a roller coaster—swooping and diving and screaming at the tight corners." [20] Ronald Hayman has only praise:

Suddenly, Arden has found absolute clarity of focus and consistency of style. For the first time, he's a master of his material. . . . It's a big and pleasant surprise that Arden manages to bring so many different characters so vividly to life, differentiating so well between them. . . . The pace is rapid, the texture is thick and the incidents are varied. . . . All through the seventeen scenes, with their profuse variety of incidents, the dramatic tension is kept taut. [21]

All the comment on the 1972 revival was favorable. Reviewers described it as "astonishingly powerful stuff" and "a warm-blooded, undogmatic and beautifully-written piece," even as "one of the best plays of the Fifties" and "one of the major plays of our time." [22]

As in *The Waters of Babylon* Arden writes, cheerfully and energetically, about low life. The difference is a greater seriousness and a greater documentary aspect. The serious side is such that the end, with injury to Sawney, the flight of Rachel, and the uncertain future of Rosie, matters more than the *death* of Krank. Arden writes in his Introductory Note that "the play is in large part meant to be funny" (101), with the comedy coming mainly from the Sawneys' goading of their respectable neighbors.

The prose again shows great enjoyment of the eloquent or unusual phrase; for example, "How'd you like a real screaming sow to raven your paunch for you?" (109); "Then home like a traction engine and revel her three times down to Rio" (111). Richard Findlater disliked "the fatal fluency of O'Casey" in "some of this prolix poeticising," [23] but such language creates the racy vigor of this piece, as Hayman argues: "His achievement in inventing a language for the

Sawneys is a very considerable one. He forges a vernacular for them which sounds illiterate but expresses everything he needs it to. It also sounds outlandish but, unlike the language in *Armstrong's Last Goodnight,* it's not difficult for the audience to understand. It's salty, often bordering on the poetic, and the crowded rhythms are like young animals in a confined space leaping for food, but they pack in the meaning breathlessly and colloquially." [24]

The Sawneys frequently sing ballad snatches, as in a latter-day *Beggars' Opera,* and, more important, nearly all the scenes are introduced with brief ballads. Arden asks that the singing of these be "dragging and harsh . . . with the peculiar monotony associated with the old fashioned street singers" (104). The object of these songs is less a Brechtian foreshadowing of the events of the scene than the conveying of some of the "poetic" themes, such as the gaiety ("Good rest and warm inside the house / For all who come along," 121) and the restricted world of the retired sailor ("you set your foot on the gangway plank / So long long time ago," 155).

Arden explains the factual origin of the play, which was "based on something which happened in Barnsley some years before, when a council house was given to a family of squatters. I didn't find out too many actual details, because I didn't want to be stuck too closely to a documentary form, but it was a similar situation, and certainly ended up like *Live Like Pigs,* with the house being besieged by the neighbours." [25] The Barnsley Housing Manager reacted with the comment that 99 percent of the town's tenants were first class, adding "We have the occasional bad tenant, as all towns have, but any allegations of immorality are without foundation, and our housewives are hard-working people with a pride in their homes." [26] The Mayor went to see the play, then stated: "I would like to see this play produced in the North, it pinpoints a problem. . . . John has certainly exaggerated the problem but the question of housing problem families is one that is faced by local authorities everywhere." [27]

Arden told me the drama was not intended to be a *Cathy Come Home* (a semi-fictional study of the housing shortage by Jeremy Sandford, much publicized when screened by B.B.C. T.V. in 1966). The Sawneys are not supposed to be typical, so he judged it unimportant that he had no firsthand knowledge of such people when he wrote it. When he moved to Kirkbymoorside, however, he was intrigued to discover that his immediate neighbors were "travelling gypsified tinkers who had ceased to travel. . . . The ones I had written about in *Live Like Pigs* were rather wilder, but the same sort of outcasts." [28] Sexual morality among these neighbors was extremely strict, but only in this respect was his dramatist's guess about such people inaccurate.

Live Like Pigs was criticized both for lack of viewpoint and for one-sidedness. Worsley writes that "what it lacks is just that thrust which a point of view would have given it." [29] For Taylor this is a virtue: "There is a determined refusal to take sides on a number of questions. . . . We may ourselves choose a side to sympathize with, if we really have to, but the choice remains ours." [30] Tynan, on the other hand, disliked the play because he found it anti-socialist, writing that *Pigs* dramatizes "the popular theory that the Welfare State destroys splendid individualism. A family . . . is shoved by officialdom into a bright new housing scheme, notable for such evidence of levelling-down as plumbing and electricity. . . . Arden's mistake . . . is to see the world outside as a world of stuffy, small-souled hypocrites, inferior simply *because* they are ordinary." [31] Similarly, Findlater found "Orwellian sentimentality about the non-bourgeoisie." [32] George Wellwarth was infuriated by Arden's treatment of the Sawneys:

To look upon people who wallow in verminous filth, disturb their neighbors with earsplitting noise, destroy their houses with wanton vandalism, and live off thievery and prostitution, as wide-eyed, innocent children of nature who deserve commiseration because the building boom has dispossessed them from their idyllic life among the flower-bedecked hedgerows is the merest muzzy-headed romanticism. [33]

While some of Wellwarth's criticism of the characters is justified—Sally is not sent to school, Col steals, Blackmouth is violent, Rachel a tart—they are not at all pictured as

"Wide-eyed, innocent children of nature." Sailor's cry, "They'll kill her. All of us. Just cos we live" (179), rouses little sympathy because Sailor boasts of being a killer too—though one may not believe all he says. Arden's achievement, however, is precisely that he makes one see how the world looks to a Sawney. Arden's emotional attachment is to the Sawneys: rationally, he knows their faults, but can still see the strengths they would display in another setting.

The first ballad in the play sings of freedom: "O England was a free country / So free beyond a doubt / That if you had no food to eat / You were free to go without" (105). The Sawneys want to be free to go without. Rachel adds a parallel ballad snatch: "For I was as free as a bird on the mountain, / For I was as free as a swallow so high" (158). When Sailor, waking in the night, looks back on his life, he speaks first of seeing "the gold and the fishes and the beasts. And the brown women. . . . New York, Archangel, Hard iron towns," then speaks of liberty: "A man can work and he gets glory, right?. . . . But after that—but after that—where is it, his glory? It's in the folk around him and his sweet liberty to hold *their* lives and glory, and stand no man's work against it. So Sawney holds the road" (156). Rachel answers "*I* got glory. . . . Like, glory of choice. Take: when I want. Choose one, choose 'em all. . . . There's choices I've had. I've made 'em. They've gone. Like, nowt. But all *mine*" (157).

She will do as the fancy takes her, unlike the circumscribed Jacksons. Mr. Jackson is a Co-operative Society van-driver and his wife says of his job, with unintentional irony, "He's like his own master" (112–13). The Sawney family was uprooted against their wishes, as Rosie tells Mrs. Jackson: "We didn't come here cos we wanted; but now we *are* here you ought to leave us be" (113). Rachel revels in their animality when she faces the mob: "We live like bloody animals, you don't know what animals are!" (178). Rosie feels persecuted like a dog: "They put us, it's like a dog in a box, you can stick spikes through every corner at him and he's no place to turn at all" (165).

Arden comments on his social attitude: "I approve outright neither of the Sawneys nor of the Jacksons. Both groups uphold standards of conduct that are incompatible, but which are both valid in their correct context" (101). He stressed to me: "It is a play about the Sawneys, not the Jacksons. Like Alan Sillitoe's *The Loneliness of the Long Distance Runner* [1959], it *is* weighted one way." His theme is conflict and its consequence that both ways of life lose "their own particular virtues under the stress of intolerance and misunderstanding" (101). This statement is misleading, for the behavior of the Sawneys inevitably arouses intolerance and misunderstanding. Only three times can one fault the Jacksons: when Mr. Jackson sleeps with Rachel, when the Jacksons assume that the assault on their daughter was entirely Col's fault, and when Mrs. Jackson too hastily blames them for the disappearance of the cat. The real fault of the Jacksons for Arden is that objects matter more than people to them. A song states this explicitly: "For their hearts are hurt and their houses hurt. / Their houses are their heart. / And those within their houses are / The least important part" (172). While the Sawneys usually appear aggressive, violence ultimately springs from the Jacksons and their friends.

Arden phrased the theme as "the difficulty of communication between very different kinds of people," which is valid, yet makes the drama sound more hackneyed than it is. As in the case of Krank, Arden avoids taking the obvious view of his characters and keeps altering the assessment of them. Scenes are kept short so that each establishes one or two aspects of the situation, and the play proceeds rapidly so as to present the varied aspects in quick succession.

Arden shows the limitations of any oversimplified view of people. The Sawneys are at first objectionable in the face of well-meaning kindness. When the persecution starts, the audience begins to sympathize, almost despite itself. The drama pleads for tolerance and understanding for even the lowest of humanity. Finally, the Sawneys are mourned as Harold Pinter's caretaker, with no place to go, was pitied. Society regrettably has no place for the Sawneys, for, if the Jacksons and their kind inherit the earth, there is little, if any, improvement. Audiences are forced to reconsider their attitudes—although Wellwarth's comment shows that he has refused to do this.

Most theatergoers are prejudiced in favor of order and good government, so Arden's picture of the Sawneys is unsettling. Arden opposes uniformity in society; he wants Sawneys and Jacksons to continue (although there must be reservations about Blackmouths and Old Croakers!). Arden fears that people inside the houses are becoming as alike as the houses are; Col describes the estate: "You got a house you got a house. Then you got a bit of garden. Then there's a house and house. Then you got a bit of garden. A house a house a bit of garden. Then you got the concrete bloody road and two blue coppers thumping up and down it. I'll tell you, I'm going off me nut already" (117).

When Is a Door Not a Door?

Another Arden play in 1958, his slightest published piece, is the one-act *When Is a Door Not a Door?* This play was commissioned by the Central School of Drama, and written and performed within a month. The requirement was to provide eleven parts of roughly equal length for a specified list of young drama students. The setting is a factory office—unusual in itself, for few write of industry. During one morning, a strike starts, personalities clash, efficient work contrasts with pointless bustle, and a gap between office and shop-floor workers is exposed. Through all the confusion two talkative workmen proceed steadily with removing and replacing a door. The chief interest of the play is that Arden thought it "completely realistic" until the director gave it the style of "a kind of *commedia dell'arte* fantasy." Arden has an affection for his play: "I enjoyed writing it, however, as a purely technical exercise, and I enjoyed seeing them do it" (11).[34]

Soldier, Soldier

Early in his career Arden wrote two television plays and also has adapted *Musgrave* for television and originally drafted *The Island of the Mighty* for the medium. He enjoys this writing "because television audiences include thousands of people who would never see one's work in the theatre, and television technique is attractive and stimulating to me"

(13). He comments however, that "I probably prefer the theatre in the long run because the finished product, if it is done well, is more satisfying than television. The trouble with television is that it is so ephemeral—the play is over in an hour. . . . You feel that on the whole television doesn't make a strong impact on people as a visit to the theatre does." [35]

He notes two significant ways in which the television audience differs: "It is not, in my opinion, correct to think of [TV] as a *mass* medium. It addresses itself, on average, to two or three people only, in their own homes, at a range of two or three yards" (9). Also, "a television audience has other channels it can turn to, it has conversation. In a theatre, if you are bored with a play you do not immediately start a conversation, but you do at home. You might keep the play on and start talking about the news, about the programme you have already seen or the day's business or anything. This is not to say that television audiences are more stupid than theatre audiences but merely that the conditions of watching the play are so different." [36]

Differences like these must be kept in mind by an author more accustomed to the theater. Because television audiences are easily distracted, Arden, in adapting *Musgrave,* found he needed to "tighten up the physical action" and judges that "if you are going to do something serious on television then you must really capture their attention at the beginning so that you can then put it over." [37] Pieces insufficiently substantial for the theater may succeed on T.V.: "There are always plays and bits of plays which one would like to write, but which seem too delicate or too unresolved for the stage. These may be themes that need another year or two to reach full fruition: but in the meanwhile, the T.V. can contain them, and their slightness will be an advantage. I mean, of course, slightness in *physique*—not in truth. . . . I myself wrote *Soldier, Soldier* for T.V.: and the following year I found that I was able to enlarge its themes to the length of *Serjeant Musgrave's Dance.*" On the subject of appropriate language in T.V. drama, he writes: "How much language can T.V. take? In general, not as much as the theatre. You cannot bawl out Englishmen in their own drawing-rooms and hope to have them listen to you next time. I have tried this in one play (*Soldier, Soldier*) but I doubt if I can repeat it. Also the gentler type of poetry tends to sound very affected at close range." [38]

Soldier, Soldier, subtitled "a comic song for television," was written in 1957 between *The Waters of Babylon* and *Live Like Pigs.* Though accepted when first submitted, the play was not screened until February, 1960, after the staging of *Musgrave* directed attention to the author. *Soldier, Soldier,* which won the Italia Prize for 1960, awarded to the best television show submitted from several European countries, concerns an unnamed Scottish private in a Northern town after he has missed his train. In a public house he learns that the son of a local family, the Scuffhams, joined his regiment and that the family has had no news of him for a long time. When he visits the Scuffham household, he pretends to be a friend of the boy and to know that he is in a military prison. The Scotsman takes over the Scuffhams' bed; seduces Mary, their Irish daughter-in-law, who still mourns her missing husband; and gets money from them by claiming it will enable him to arrange a re-trial. After a few days, when he has to return to the army, Mary wants to accompany him; but he refuses her and goes toward the railroad station. In a final scene in the public house a neighbor of the Scuffhams charges the private with lying, which he freely admits, but he strides away singing after paying for drinks all round.

Though the description is "a *comic* song," *Soldier, Soldier* is foremost a sad little story about simple, pathetically ignorant people who are deceived. But, as usual with Arden, the work is less straightforward, for, as Irving Wardle has noted, the townsfolk are a caricature: "the dwarfish figures, with their drooping moustaches and shapeless clothes, stand out grotesquely like Brueghel's misshapen peasants." [39] Arden exaggerates the dreary, lifeless daily round of many people in such passages as this: "Well, it wor a lovely tea, I made her a lovely tea. There was chips from around the corner, and a bit of pork-pie fried, and treacle we had, and a lovely yellow cake bought special, and she wouldn't take a bite. It's downright criminal, all that good shop food goes to waste" (32).

The Scuffhams and their neighbors resemble the Jacksons of *Live Like Pigs* and Petey and Meg of Pinter's *Birthday Party.* The Scuffhams are narrow-minded Nonconformists, teetotalers, and Sabbatarians. The Scots soldier's visit rouses Mary, the Irish girl, to leave her stultifying English home with the Scuffhams; and he provides both energy and excitement for a few moments for the men, "mostly elderly and nondescript," in the "dreary little working-class tavern" (18). The soldier, who calls himself "a randy chancer" ("randy" is a common term for lecherous), is a likable scoundrel similar to Krank. He represents Arden's view of the essential characteristics of the private soldier, just as the soldier in *The Royal Pardon* does, by combining the toughness of Hurst and the vitality of Sparky of *Musgrave.* This quintessential aspect of the soldier gives the play the quality of a ballad or fable; it is not just an account of a confidence trick but a good-humored generalized warning against gullibility that recalls Arden's admiration for Ben Jonson.

The title comes from a well-known folk song about a girl who is so eager to marry a soldier that she gives him all he asks for, only to learn finally that he is already married. The tune is played several times, usually by the soldier on a penny-whistle (which Mary succeeds in taking from him), and snatches are also sung. Nearly half the play is in verse; and Arden has explained that, "In *Soldier, Soldier,* the experiment was to try to see if verse was a possibility on the small screen. . . . I do not believe that *Soldier, Soldier,* justified itself as a verse play" (9, 10). The verse is unmistakeably Arden's—brief, direct, elemental, as when Mary and the soldier speak of their evening out together:

> Mary: Like rainfall or like snow they fall / Words are
>   black / Or words are white.
> Soldier: *Now* you'd say black: / Last evening, naked white.
>   (67–68)

The poetry is one of several strengths of this satisfying work. To the verse can be added the use of ballads and music; the atmosphere of pub, chapel, and of the "typical

street in a colliery town . . . a general air of muck without
much money" (38); the comment on the restricted lives of
many; the complex character of Mary; the vivid portrait of
the soldier; and the brisk unfolding of the story.

Wet Fish

Wet Fish, written after *The Business of Good Government*
and screened in September, 1961, is linked loosely with
Soldier, Soldier, through its setting in a Northern town. The
play begins in an architect's office, headed by the Yorkshireman, Gilbert Garnish, "a frenzied little round ball of energy"
(83).[40] His four assistants include Ruth, a newly qualified
architect, and Krank (previously seen in *The Waters of
Babylon*), still leading a double life involving Teresa and
mysterious long-distance phone calls in Polish. Although
Garnish is involved in many substantial projects and is frequently away from town, he undertakes the reconstruction
of a fish shop, which he had originally designed twenty years
earlier. Ruth, who is placed in charge of the project, soon experiences unforeseen difficulties; the builder takes advantage
of her inexperience; and problems, anger, and expenses
mount. Finally, the fishmonger is ready to sell his shop to
Krank and become a tenant, for Krank has secretly bought
the properties on either side. Krank himself is fired by Garnish, but he persuades Ruth to go and live with him.

Since Arden describes the play as "an attempt to present
on the screen a fictional version of one of my own experiences during the two years I spent as an inefficient assistant
in an architect's office," this work is the closest he has ever
come to autobiography. When discussing *Wet Fish,* he explained "I wrote the play deliberately in a flat and natural-
istic manner—having learnt something from *Soldier,
Soldier*—in the hope that it would prove possible to use the
documentary potential of the television medium to give
greater vividness to my main theme" (10). Arden intended,
therefore, an element of experiment; but some aspects of the
play were to be resolved in discussion with the director and
at the rehearsals. Parts were written for particular actors,
and Arden hoped that "a use of architect's plans and models,

combined with realistic shots of the building work itself, would assist and, in some sequences, replace the dialogue" (10). But these hopes were not fulfilled because a director was appointed who showed no interest in even meeting Arden, let alone cooperating with him at rehearsals; and, as a result, Arden was angered by the way *Wet Fish* was played and by the attitude of television companies toward authors.

Nevertheless, he rightly concludes that the play "worked quite well as a straight situation comedy" (11). Often, the play is farce rather than comedy when the builders carry into the fish shop "enormous quantities" of material; the office tea-man is "a decrepit old skiver," a work dodger who "totters" about grumbling; and the foreman is a "deep-eyed pessimist" who is given such lines as "continued disappointment is the lot of the human race" (118). Apart from the laughs, *Wet Fish* has—like *When Is a Door Not a Door?*—the unusual subject of men at work; and Frederick Laws praised "the atmosphere of low endeavour, frustration, and sour joking among the well-intentioned and down-trodden juniors who did the work." [41] A general atmosphere of intrigue is developed when the tea-man pesters Garnish for easier working conditions, the foreman attempts to get Ruth to help him change his job, and Garnish tries to negotiate a slightly shady deal over the damaged foundations in the cathedral's Lady Chapel. The corruption that is ever present, usually just out of sight, involves a deal over lunch at a club, not trying to obtain the lowest tender, or employing a contractor because his brother is going to be Chairman of the Housing Committee. The dry rot in the fish shop and the business immorality led Angus Wilson to see the piece as a metaphor of "the rotting structure of English social life." [42]

Just as *When Is a Door* was written as realism and became fantasy in production, *Wet Fish* was written as documentary experiment and became realism in performance. Despite slight unorthodoxies (the mystery around Krank, and once again the use of a tune—"When father papered the parlour"—as *leitmotif*), *Wet Fish* is as straightforward and commercial a play as Arden has ever written.

Chapter Three
Serjeant Musgrave's Dance

The Plot and its Difficulties

Serjeant Musgrave's Dance, subtitled "an unhistorical parable," is Arden's most discussed and controversial drama. Although *Musgrave* resembles *Soldier, Soldier* because it focuses on Army deserters who come to a Northern industrial town, the stage play is set in Victorian times. The exact date is not given, but Arden had in mind his hometown of Barnsley as it was between 1860 and 1880. These years saw the early struggles of miners' unions when troops were garrisoned in Northern towns to keep order.

The drama begins with four soldiers on a canal wharf who play cards while waiting for a barge to take them and their equipment to a nearby town. They are led by Serjeant Musgrave, a cold, stern, and deeply religious man. The privates are middle-aged Attercliffe, kind yet melancholy; young Sparky, full of silly jokes and "easily led, easily driven;"[1] and moody, surly Hurst. The Bargee, who takes them to town, is noisy, ugly, and contemptuous of soldiers; he subsequently links most of the action, which occurs during two exceptionally cold winter days.

The second of the eight scenes is in an inn: Mrs. Hitchcock, the landlady, an austere though understanding widow, is talking to the parson about the colliers' strike which grips the town. When the soldiers arrive, they say they have come seeking recruits and the mayor sees that they could usefully enlist some of the strikers' leaders. Musgrave arranges to have a bed in the inn and for the other three to sleep in the stable. He startles Mrs. Hitchcock by mentioning Billy Hicks,

34

a townsman who joined the army, leaving the barmaid Annie pregnant, and was soon killed overseas.

In a churchyard, the setting for the next scene, the soldiers assess the town and reveal that they are deserters. They have come to avenge Hicks's needless death, "to work that guilt back to where it began" (34). When Musgrave is asked how this is to be done, he speaks cryptically of God and dances. Their deliberations are interrupted by three colliers, who fear the troops have been sent as strikebreakers.

The fourth scene returns to the inn, where the Bargee dances and Sparky sings, performs card tricks, and beats a drum. Annie, who says she is "whoor-to-the-soldiers—it's a class by itself" (60), tells Hurst that she will visit him that night, and rejects Sparky's overtures. In the short street scene that follows, the Bargee, as preparation for enlisting, tries to drill two of the miners in what is half a drunken game and half a serious act. The Bargee suggests to them that they steal the soldiers' Gatling gun.

The three privates prepare to sleep in the stable in the sixth scene. Annie comes to Hurst, who rejects her; Sparky comforts her, then impulsively suggests that they run away together. At this point, Musgrave, in his room across the courtyard, has a nightmare in which he is apparently God presiding over the end of the world; Mrs. Hitchcock calms him. Arden explains that this incident "should make the audience shudder and that's all that's intended." When Hurst sees Sparky is preparing to leave, he rushes to stop him and in the scuffle Attercliffe accidentally kills Sparky. In a flurry of activity the Bargee arrives with the news that the colliers are stealing the gun, and they rush out and catch the leader, Walsh. The mayor, fearing riots, summons dragoons from a nearby town.

In the recruiting meeting in the marketplace that follows, the mayor and the parson praise army life. Musgrave demonstrates the use of the Gatling gun, then surprises them by hoisting a skeleton in uniform on the flagpost. Musgrave sings and dances, waving his rifle, then covers the astonished mayor, parson, and constable with the gun. He tells them that the corpse is that of Billy Hicks, and he describes the atrocity in a colony for which the soldiers had been partly responsible. Musgrave's mission is apparently complete, but he surprises them; for, because five were killed in the colony, he declares that they must kill twenty-five here. Annie enters, bringing Sparky's bloodstained tunic, and her news makes Walsh turn against the troops. The panicky Hurst prepares to shoot at the crowd, but Attercliffe stands in front of the gun. The dei ex machina, the dragoons, arrive now, shooting Hurst and arresting the two survivors. Annie lowers the skeleton and cradles it, while the rest drink beer and then link hands and dance around her. Arden explains this moment: "The audience should be made conscious of the fact that the town has been taken over by the real military—the dragoons. . . . Even the most sympathetic of the colliers, who nearly sides with Musgrave, has no alternative but to take part in the dance." [2]

In the final scene Mrs. Hitchcock visits Musgrave and Attercliffe in prison, and encourages them to think that some day their message will be heeded. Attercliffe moralizes, "You can't cure the pox by further whoring" (102), and concludes with a tentative hint of hope, "D'you reckon we can start an orchard?" (104) When I asked Arden if this final image was an optimistic touch, he replied: "This is Attercliffe speaking, not Arden, and anyway, it's questioning, not assertive. Attercliffe balances the cynicism of the town dancing. Because Musgrave has despaired, Attercliffe has to have the last line. The play is fiction, so there is no reason for it to end positively; were it about the Tolpuddle Martyrs it would have an agitprop, hopeful ending."

Serjeant Musgrave's Dance was first performed at the Royal Court Theater in October, 1959, with Ian Bannen playing Musgrave. There was support for only twenty-eight performances, and the production lost £5,820, more than the Court's total annual subsidy from the Arts Council. During the next two years the play was performed by many university groups, and the Leeds University and Lincoln Repertory Company productions led many critics who first disliked the play to praise it. A television performance, with Patrick McGoohan in the title role, followed in October, 1961. Two years later Peter Brook directed the drama in Paris with Laurent Terzieff in the lead. The major reviews were bad, and next day the audience was only five. So three free performances were announced; they were crowded. Lengthy discussions onstage after the show were led by Arthur Adamov, Jean-Luc Godard, and Alain Resnais. *Musgrave* was revived at the Royal Court at the end of 1965, and again in May, 1977 for a provincial tour starting in Oxford, with Donal McCann as the serjeant. American productions include the Actors' Workshop, San Francisco (1962); the Theater de Lys in New York (March, 1966, for 135 performances); the Arena Stage, Washington, D.C. (April, 1966); Minnesota (June, 1968); C.S.C. Repertory, New York (December, 1977); and in numerous universities, among them Villanova, where a black played the lead, adding new meaning to "*Black* Jack Musgrave." In May, 1981 there was a third major London production at the Cottesloe, when John Burgess directed John Thaw in the title role. *Musgrave* was awarded the *Encyclopaedia Britannica* prize in 1959 and the Vernon Rice award in 1966.

Analysis

The initial critical reception was largely hostile. Harold Hobson in the *Sunday Times* dismissed the play as "another frightful ordeal," [3] and Eric Keown asked in *Punch*: "Why was this piece put on? A play that was anti-Empire and anti-Army would conceivably have its appeal in Sloane Square [the address of the Royal Court], but surely not one that was eighty years out of date? If a tract was wanted on those lines it could have been written more persuasively by an intelligent child. . . . There might have been some felicities of dialogue or wit to leaven this lump of absurdity, but I failed to detect them." [4]

Incomprehension when faced with a difficult and unusual play was excusable in the earliest reviewers, but hostility continued. George Wellwarth saw only "a clumsily written case study of a lunatic. . . . Arden's play [is] exasperating and, in the last analysis, uninteresting." [5] Hilary Spurling wrote of the 1965 revival that "it works on such a crude and childish level that the whole problem [of the use of force] is reduced to absurdity. . . . I defy anyone to explain the plot,

except perhaps as a series of expedients to stave off the
grand climax until the last act. . . . Muddle runs through the
whole play and by the end has reached truly startling pro-
portions." [6] *Time*'s critic, at the off-Broadway premiére,
noted one much-too-obvious meaning: "He has managed to
fulminate for very nearly three hours on General Sherman's
admirably succinct text: War is hell." [7] Those who believe,
with Martin Esslin, that this is "one of the finest plays produced in this country in this century," [8] have much to
answer.

Lindsay Anderson, the director, started the movement that
favored the play, which he judged one of "extraordinary
talent and originality," [9] by producing a flier in which
various theater people praised *Musgrave*. John Osborne, for
example, wrote: "Arden's play has more riches to offer than
a dozen successful, dazzling critic-comforters. It is
courageous, theatrically adventurous and it has startling
integrity." [10]

Arden himself concluded that reviewers were too sophisticated: "Audiences (and particularly critics) find it hard to
make the completely simple response to the story that is the
necessary preliminary to appreciating the meaning of the
play." [11] He also admitted, "I have a feeling that there is
something wrong with *Serjeant Musgrave's Dance*. I have
never been able to put my finger on it. I have asked lots of
people for their ideas on this and they have all suggested different things. . . . Somehow I have not managed to balance
the business of giving the audience information so that they
can understand the play with the business of withholding information in order to keep the tension going." [12]

The most common criticism is of the length and complexity of the first six scenes, making up two of the three acts, of
which Hobson said: "It is quite impossible to discover what
it is that Mr. Arden has to tell, let alone whether it matters or
not." [13] Albert Bermel is bewildered by these acts because
"the exposition . . . unravels forward and backward at the
same time, explaining and rehearsing motives while it un-
covers new matter, so that the past clogs up the present." [14]
Arden replies: "What I was doing in *Musgrave* was using two
acts for what is commonly done in one, in most three-act

plays. I don't see that this is necessarily wrong." [15] By this he means that he is very gradually unfolding the soldiers' past and their intentions, and painting a full picture of the town and its inhabitants. Arden is ready to fault the third scene: "The general purpose of the soldiers' visit should be made much clearer. The real trouble is that in the churchyard scene, where they explain themselves, there is a tremendous amount of emotion being generated. They are all getting angry with each other, and Musgrave goes off into a religious tirade. The result is that the audience is so busy watching the actors dramatising their emotions that they aren't picking up the plot information which is being conveyed in the dialogue." [16]

The prompt copy shows a number of simplifications and clarifications in the first production. Annie is less enigmatic when her lines, "But it drowned three score of sailors, and the King of Norway's daughter" (51) and "All round his hat he wore the green willow" (59) are cut. Her speech near the end, "My truth's an easy tale, it's old true-love gone twisted, like they called it 'malformed,' " (95) is rewritten in a simpler form. Her descent in this scene by what the Bargee calls "a gold staircase" is gone. In Musgrave's prayer at the end of the churchyard scene "greater" is substituted for "worse" in "The Word alone is terrible: the Deed must be worse," an improvement since "worse" misleads audiences about what to expect later. In the opening scene an additional "Heard who laugh?" from Hurst makes a little clearer the fact that the box contains a corpse, while the addition of Mrs. Hitchcock repeating "Billy Hicks" to herself at the very end of the second scene emphasizes the name for its later importance.[17]

Arden made changes for the television version: "I tried not to simplify any of the moral complications and ambiguity which are deliberate in the play. . . . We did . . . tighten up the physical action. I somewhat modified Serjeant Musgrave's own psychology. I think I made him a little bit clearer as a person." [18] In the revision (not published) Arden identifies Musgrave more directly with wheels than with logic and the book. With a pit-wheel visible behind the churchyard, Musgrave says their plan is "to bring the wheel

round." After Sparky's death Musgrave looks into the box at
Hicks's skeleton and declaims "The wheel of Your logic shall
be brought round spoke by spoke without deluding mercy."
The character of Musgrave can indeed be clarified and explanations be given earlier. While the stage text states enough
for perceptive readers and audiences, the television script
eliminates some difficulties and explains others. Running 84
minutes, primarily it is an abridgment (less is revealed about
the three privates, for example), showing what Arden finds
most important.

Ronald Bryden, reviewing in the *New Statesman,* identifies two flaws in the drama. First, he considers that the killing
of Sparky dislocates the "sure flow" and "sense of reality,"
and that its impact is muffled by "a flurry of melodramatic
comings and goings." However, the tension of the situation,
with all the soldiers scared, uncertain, and desperate, and
Hurst especially unsettled at this point, is such as to make
violence almost inevitable. While the flurry that follows is
realistic, not melodramatic, it does tend to distract from
Sparky's death, which is unfortunate as his death is crucial to
the turn of events next day in the marketplace. The television version places earlier both the colliers' attempt to steal
the Gatling gun and the news that the dragoons are on their
way, thus reducing the rush of events in the few minutes
following the killing of Sparky. Second, Bryden writes of the
last scene that "what commences with the power and sure-
ness of a legend or ballad peters out in discussion." [19] In fact,
this scene is the only time in the play in which cool discussion of the events—commentary rather than activity—takes
place. Mrs. Hitchcock and Attercliffe are more explicit than
they are anywhere else and show how they are affected by
what occurred at the meeting: the landlady is still kindly,
Attercliffe confused, Musgrave confused *and* despairing.

The criticism most in need of an answer is Hilary
Spurling's: "Musgrave holds up the town at gun point in the
market place. Why? What does he hope to gain by it?" [20]
Musgrave's own view is "What happens afterwards, the Lord
God will provide. I am with you, He said" (36). Like Hurst,
he also wants to kill the leaders, "them that sent it [madness]
out of this country" (92). "We've *got* to be remembered!"

(94), Musgrave says, by a big enough atrocity in England, not in some faraway colony, which could start a nationwide revulsion against violence, militarism, and colonialism. The adaptation for television changes the plan to the taking of hostages, so anxiety about what is to happen replaces puzzling for the audience. When Musgrave first meets the mayor, he asks if there are many "solid citizens left in residence, like tradesmen and such. Maybe five and twenty?" Then, in the churchyard scene, Musgrave says that their recruiting meeting must "glamorize them with the glory," and Attercliffe explains that they should "detach 25, hold them under guard, say 'This is what we've gone and done—these are the hostages. We're holding them to ransom.' We say that to the town and we say it to the whole country. The newspapers, Parliament. What about the Queen? If you will save these 25, you'll all save yourselves. To stop the killings. Stop it. And that's how it will happen." Finally, in the marketplace scene Musgrave takes the keys of the town jail from the constable, arrests him with the mayor and the parson, and demands "I want 22 more of the same mind and station who are in the town. Who'll settle for it?"

Essentially, though, the four men are confused and have varied purposes, and this indicates the main themes. "You can't cure the pox by further whoring"—violence cannot end violence—is in fact examined in several important aspects: why the pox at all? can it be cured in any way? who is qualified to attempt the cure?

In considering "why the pox?" Arden includes several quite familiar answers. The mayor and parson, the Establishment, are ready to use force at home in breaking the strike and, in general, as in the parson's speech: "When called to shoulder our country's burdens we should do it with a glancing eye and a leaping heart, to draw the sword with gladness, thinking nothing of our petty differences and grievances—but all united under one brave flag, going forth in Christian resolution" (79). Musgrave and his men demonstrate an unthinking readiness to carry out orders, and the Bargee and some of the colliers are ready to follow whichever leader holds power. Hurst and a miner show aggression, and even Attercliffe, the mildest man present, has a moment of anger (49).

While touching on motives that cause wars, Arden gives much more attention to the less familiar topic of the motives of pacifists, the question of "who should attempt the cure?" His Introduction hints that this is his major concern: "I would suggest, however, that a study of the roles of the women, and of Private Attercliffe, should be sufficient to remove any doubts as to where the 'moral' of the play lies. . . . Complete pacifism is a very hard doctrine: and if this play appears to advocate it with perhaps some timidity, it is probably because I am naturally a timid man—and also because I know that if I am hit I very easily hit back: and I do not care to preach too confidently what I am not sure I can practise" (7). The limitations of the men themselves are the main reason for their failure. Attercliffe is the complete pacifist, asserting "all wars is sin" and "they've got to turn against all wars" (33, 36).

He ultimately is the one who understands nonviolence, putting himself in front of Musgrave's gun. He now finds soldiering dishonorable, while Musgrave remains proud of his markmanship. Musgrave objects only to the particular war in which he was involved, and brushes aside Attercliffe's absolutism in the churchyard scene. Attercliffe is shaped more by his wife's unfaithfulness than by Billy Hicks's death. Sparky's pacifism is an unthinking reaction to his friend's death, and aggression that is barely repressed is prominent in both Musgrave and Hurst.

Hurst's shortcomings suggest that pacifists are sometimes unwise in those whom they accept as allies. None of the privates is sufficiently dedicated: drink and lust lead to the fight in the stable and Sparky's death. Though this is accidental, these confused and angry men are inadequate to lead the world to new, worthier standards. Thus Arden suggests that pacifist motives may sometimes be suspect and that pacifists may lack self-knowledge, especially of the savagery that can underlie nonviolent theory. The soldiers' uncertain relations with authorities and colliers, and the lack of plan at the marketplace gathering, further show pacifists as unsure about what they are trying to do, inadequately understanding the complexities of the world. In discussing this theme of pacifists' motives, Arden said that while he thought each would-be pacifist was likely to become rather like Musgrave or Sparky or Attercliffe, the play referred less to kinds of pacifists than to the internal debate that pacifists should have.

The barmaid Annie completes the picture of the consequences of force. At the end of the marketplace scene she is on the platform in the center of the stage, cradling the skeleton of her dead lover. Although she is indirectly responsible for two deaths, of Billy Hicks and Sparky, she finally is the suffering victim. And so her love is "an old true-love gone twisted, like they called it 'malformed' " (95). She mourns both her dead—Sparky perhaps more than the earlier one—and rejects all Musgrave's ideas of revenge. Even Musgrave is impressed: "She talks a kind of truth, that lassie. Is she daft?" (26).

Another woman also chooses life: Attercliffe's unseen wife rightly rejected a soldier to choose the useful, productive greengrocer, who "fed the people" (61) (similarly Mrs. Hitchcock thinks that when the colliers are fed, they will be ready to heed Musgrave's message). Cuckolding is another kind of threat to established order.

A closely related idea is that colonial war may be used unconsciously by a nation to export internal violence. This notion is mentioned directly when the authorities suggest to Musgrave that he recruit the most troublesome strikers, and appears more vividly as the soldiers' infection with a madness they have brought back. Hurst speaks forcefully in the churchyard: "We're wild-wood mad and raging. We caught it overseas and now we've got to run around the English streets biting every leg to give it *them*" (36). Musgrave develops the theme of soldiers infected with madness in his marketplace speeches: "Now there's a disease. . . . Wild-wood mad we are; and so we've fetched it home" (90). Addressing Walsh, he continues, "Join along with my madness, friend. I brought it back to England but I've brought the cure too—to turn it on to them that sent it out of this country—way-out-ay they sent it, where they hoped that only soldiers could catch it and rave!" (92). Ironically, though Musgrave can diagnose violence as madness, it has made him close to madness himself. Arden has wondered if American involvement in Vietnam and British action in Cyprus and Aden were partly designed to expel potential internal violence. Musgrave and his men do bring bloodlust back with them: Walsh, as well as the elite of the town, is ready to use a gun.

A society prepared to use violence requires Authority, which raises a theme found also in *Live Like Pigs* and later plays, the desirability of freedom and the necessity of order. The earlier play shows humane facets of order in the well-intentioned housing official and the final ambulance bell. The representatives of order in *Musgrave* are less sympathetic: the mayor, who wants to protect his profits and property, and Musgrave, obsessed with "my duty. Good order and the discipline: it's the only road I know" (102). Musgrave's words contrast with the words, *life, love,* and *anarchy.* The point is made also through the image of a book, and scribbling on it. Musgrave talks constantly of acting by the book: "You give [your life] to your people, for peace, and for honesty. . . . That's *my* book. . . . I'm the Queen of England's man, . . . and I know her Book backwards. . . . The Queen's Book, which eighteen years I've lived" (83–84, 90). The Bible is also a book of Queen's Rules for him. Musgrave warns Annie not to visit the men: "There's work is for women and there's work is for men: and let the two get mixed, you've anarchy. . . . Look, lassie, anarchy: now, we're soldiers. Our work isn't easy, no and it's not soft: it's got a strong name—duty. And it's drawn out straight and black for us, a clear plan. But if you come to us with what you call your life or love—*I'd* call it your indulgence—and you scribble all over that plan, you make it crooked, dirty, idle, untidy, *bad*—there's anarchy" (51).

In the last scene, in which Arden comes as close as he ever does to explicit conclusions, Mrs. Hitchcock tells Musgrave that what he attempted was also anarchy; and that he failed because he did not see the life and love in the town. She says that despite strikes, cold, and repression: "Here we are, and we'd got life and love. Then *you* came in and you did your scribbling where nobody asked you. Aye, it's arsy-versey to what you said, but it's still an anarchy, isn't it?" (102).

Musgrave and his men, paradoxically, have carried out an

anarchic act in deserting. Sparky's decision to seek happiness by running away with Annie deliberately rejects Musgrave and his doctrines: "It *wouldn't* be anarchy, you know; he can't be right there! All it would be, is: *you* live and *I* live—we don't need his duty, we don't need his Word—a dead man's a dead man! We could call it *all* paid for! Your life and my life—make our *own* road" (63–64). So Sparky surrenders to instinct and is killed for it: peace and love are unattainable for him. People—as in the little kindnesses of Mrs. Hitchcock and the pathetic figure of Annie—matter and abstractions do not. Humanity is not all good, however: the devious Bargee, who changes direction according to the wind, like Michael Finnegan's whiskers of which he sings, may be more dangerous in his unscrupulousness than Musgrave's known inflexible purposes.[21] Life is a muddle, a fact Arden finds inconvenient *and* fortunate. In the muddle is a place for sadness and happiness, and Musgrave ignores the demands of life and love—which he should not want to change.

The theme of life and love struggling for an outlet in an unsympathetic setting relates to the theme of loneliness. Arden spoke of the problem of communication in *Live Like Pigs,* and refers to this again when he writes that because Sparky "is making jokes all the time there must be a failure in communication between him and everybody else. Because you cannot carry on a complete relationship in the form of jokes." [22] Sparky's loneliness is established at the very beginning, where he stands on guard alone while Hurst and Attercliffe play cards beside a lantern. Annie, too, obviously desperately seeks consolation for her loneliness. Musgrave is equally isolated, and the third scene shows this fact when he prays alone after the men have left the churchyard.[23]

Musgrave, however, chooses to be solitary, a part of his singleness of mind, his "purity," as Richard Gilman terms it.[24] Arden explores the merits and failings of singleness of purpose, as Charles Morgan does in a neglected play, *The Flashing Stream* (1938). The privates fight in the stable and disagree in the marketplace partly because they lack Musgrave's determination.

On the other hand, Attercliffe can see that their purity is

destroyed by Sparky's death—"Don't you see, that wipes the whole thing out, wiped out, washed out, finished" (73)—which Musgrave refuses to see. Similarly, Musgrave cannot comprehend why the merits of his plan are not apparent to others; nor can he see what went wrong. He dismisses any fact he prefers not to face with his favorite phrase, "It's not material." Musgrave is enslaved by his purpose (and by his faith, as he understands it), just as the community is determined by its environment.[25] After his nightmare he has difficulty in holding to his position, and his speeches to Mrs. Hitchcock (65) are an apologetic, defensive confession, an emotional attempt to persuade himself and her, pleading "You *do* understand me, don't you?"

The meaning of Musgrave's dance is hard to grasp. It is a metaphor for his "cure," his propitiation, his arrangement with God; in its performance it symbolizes his whole mission. The words he sings state his paradox: because no one knows who is ultimately to blame for the boy's death, he will always haunt these people's memories; because no direct blame can be laid for war, it is everyone's fault. Perhaps the dance itself is a parody of the morning drill-parade, an echo of Musgrave's failure as a recruit to hear commands properly (65–66). As he dances, he is metaphorically halfway across the parade ground alone—not because he did not hear the commands, but because he hears different commands.

The dance is also a ritual with biblical parallels. Both as God's representative and as the Queen's his dancing recalls King David in his dance before the Ark (I Chron. 15:28, 29), another dance which was wholly misunderstood by the spectators. Both are warriors executing a long-forgotten ritual before a holy relic (the skeleton); both are symbols of authority; both have a new order in mind. The dance also attempts to reproduce the conditions of which it is symbolic, like the Communion of the Last Supper. The dance takes place among surroundings chosen or arranged to fit the circumstances of the original killing of the five innocent natives: the original victim is there; the colliers are close to revolt, like the natives; the mayor and parson resemble the officers who ordered Billy's killers to be found; the same soldiers are there, intending to apply more military logic.

Other associations are macabre jokes, with the dance parodying the jerky movements of the skeleton as it is pulled
from the box: both wear red tunics and perform a dance of
death.[26] Musgrave hangs Billy, anticipating his own hanging;
at his own hanging he may dance at the end of a rope.
Musgrave's dance to God and the ritual of slaughter contrasts
with the general dance at the end of the scene, which suggests a celebration of the approach of Spring[27] and the feeling that the dragoons have "saved" them, though Mrs.
Hitchcock comments that "it's not a dance of joy" (102).
This dance suggests that collective action is not the
answer—any solution must be on a personal level.

Hobson's review emphasized Musgrave as a mad god:
Musgrave's voice is that of "a God that has gone out of his
mind. . . . The quiet, muted ending of the play, when Musgrave, manacled and in prison, stands silently with his back
to the audience, is one of its finest achievements. . . . He is,
for the first time, bewildered; and for the first time we cannot see his face. It is not for us to look upon a god,
humiliated."[28] Arden, on the other hand, stresses that Musgrave is "a plausible historical type . . . one of those Crimean Sergeants, who fought with rifle in one hand, and bible
in the other."[29] He added to me that "Musgrave is a product
of moral confusion, of a country that relies on war as a
means of solving its problems. But obviously he is not rational in the crazy logic he produces."

Musgrave embodies the Nonconformist conscience, with
its stress on the individual relating directly to God. The more
extreme, rigid forms of Evangelical religion, which fascinate
Arden, appeared also in Anthract in *The Life of Man,* the
Scuffhams in *Soldier, Soldier,* and the wandering preachers
in *Armstrong* and in *Ironhand.* Musgrave, having convinced
himself that he is to carry out God's work, finally sees himself almost as God: Sparky is only half joking when he calls
Musgrave "God." Musgrave's religious preoccupations have
traces of John Bunyan or George Fox, and his need to dance
can best be understood in terms of Fox's Lichfield vision or
the eagerness of some churches for "speaking in tongues."
Though Musgrave's faith is important, so is his profession.
Eighteen years of giving orders in the army make him obsessed

with order, so that he starts believing his own logic can solve any problem and that he can give commands to the whole world.

In addition, his guilt for the colonial atrocity blends with his earnest Christianity and his authoritarianism to produce both the argument for killing twenty-five townspeople and the inadequacy of his whole plan. He broods on the sources of war, hoping to find some truth by the return to Billy Hicks's hometown, and is unsettled by his failure to discover answers. Musgrave never sees that his means—threats and killings—contradict his peaceful ends. If Musgrave finally is mad, he is no madder than British World War I generals who ordered continual pointless and costly attacks. His is the madness of which wars are made: his talk of the logic of twenty-five eyes for five eyes comments on the arguments that help to bring about wars, and this demand for more deaths suggests the effect his many years of legalized killing have had on him. Jack Richardson, American playwright and *Commentary* critic, convincingly refutes the "case-history of a lunatic" view of the play: "Consider the problem Musgrave has set about to solve. On our planet it allows of no reasonable solution, and trying to discover one—indeed, being passionately committed to its discovery—leads, through the maze of obstacles the world can set up against someone out to keep it from a self-extinction, past rational boundaries to desperate acts. Musgrave may, like the young men who incinerate themselves to protest a war, be mad, but what is sanity's alternative?" [30]

Sanity's alternative might be the nonviolence of a strike (or it may be a lockout), but the colliers lack confidence in this method and attempt to steal the gun. However, Walsh, ringleader in this attempt, is anti-military (90–91) and confused (92) after Musgrave's revelations, and he may be more of a convert to pacifism than his remark "We're back where we were" suggests. Arden agrees with critics who observed that the role of the workers should be more developed: "The leader of the trade union is built up in the first half, and then the soldiers dominate. It is a failure in dramatic construction."

The mayor, parson, and constable are types rather than rounded characters, just as the colliers are. Arden describes his technique with these figures as "silhouettes." Taking the mayor as an example, he explains: "I've purely emphasized in the mayor those aspects of the man's character that deal with his attitude to the coal industry and his attitude to the military. His attitude to his wife or to the education of his children or anything like that is completely outside the purpose of the play. . . . It's a missing-out of details rather than an exaggeration of features." [31] The parson is "the representative of the Established Church, in itself a frustrating circumstance. So one can't expect him to debate earnestly with Musgrave."

Though several charaters may appear to be cardboard Toytown figures, Arden succeeds in showing the different classes and different attitudes with only nine townspeople. The middle class finally joins together with some of the proletarians in the chain dance in rejecting the outsiders.

The play invites a mythic-allegorical approach. Attercliffe, playing cards in the first scene, speaks of throwing over the Red Queen, and under her auspices Musgrave, the Black *Jack,* who has just journeyed across water, seeks to kill the Beast of War. He retreats to a Cave of Despair, the inn, has a vision of the end of the world, and is resuscitated by grog and biscuits proferred by Mrs. Hitchcock, the sibylline, wise mother figure. His quest is endangered and finally thwarted by the Enchantress, Annie, a witch who has brought forth a monster from her womb (a deformed baby, which died about the time Hicks was killed, 27). She leaves the inn by descending what the Bargee calls "a golden staircase" (91), which symbolically connects heaven and earth. Attercliffe is the wise old man who assists the hero and repulses the advances of the seductress, and his wife and the greengrocer represent the Garden or Orchard. The quest fails, but its cyclical nature is emphasized by the thaw, the restoration of order by the dragoons, and the possibility of the apple seed. There are ironic reversals: Musgrave is both hero and victim of the Beast. Arden, like Edmund Spenser, appears to have found the symbols ready-made to his hand and evolved his characters as aspects of a shared experience.

The inspiration and sources of the play are numerous. First, Arden realized that the *Soldier, Soldier* situation could be developed. *Musgrave,* he told the *Encore* interviewers, was "a definite follow-through of the same story idea . . . the same setting, a colliery town and the arrival of a soldier. . . . There is the same relationship with the girl, or something approaching it. There is the air of violence from the outside world coming in on a closed community." [32] In addition, various details are similar: a girl dangles a soldier-doll on a string, the plot turns on a local boy who enlists and does not return, soldiers dominate customers in a public-house scene.

Second, Arden was roused to anger by reports of the violence used by British soldiers in Famagusta, Cyprus, on October 3, 1958: "One of the things that set the play off was an incident in Cyprus. A soldier's wife was shot in the street by terrorists—and according to newspaper reports—which was all I had to work on at the time—some soldiers ran wild at night and people were killed in the rounding-up." The interviewer pointed out, "In the Cyprus incident, five people died, one of them a little girl, as in your play," and Arden replied, "That was quite deliberate." [33] The description of the atrocity given by the soldiers toward the climax of the recruiting meeting (86–87) is similar to the Cyprus events.

A statement in the program of the 1965 London revival related the drama to later conflicts:

Please don't attach too much weight to the drama critic of *The Times* who says "When [this play] first appeared, its sidelong references to the Cyprus troubles over-shadowed the main content. . . . The action has now settled into legend." Cyprus may be a solved problem. May be. Aden? Malaysia? Do I have to list them? Rhodesia was once a Victorian Imperialist adventure. Vietnam has never been a *British* colony, of course, but . . . 1965–6 is as ugly a year's end as was 1958–9, when this play was conceived and written. I propose to give all my royalties from this production to the Christian Action funds for relief of political prisoners in South Africa. Because South Africa is the worst reminder we have of those historical grandfathers of ours who sent the "legendary" Serjeant Musgrave and his men off to the wars. [34]

This passage shows that Arden is desperately anxious that audiences should look for continued topical significance in

Musgrave, and not dismiss it because the nature of the problems of Cyprus changed. Similarly, in 1980 he suggests a different frame of reference for the drama: "I wrote a play
attacking the complacency with which the British public was
prepared to regard actions undertaken by the British Army in
foreign parts. The play becomes famous. It is presented as an
examination piece for schoolchildren. And the British Army
continues to do exactly the same things in Ireland, and has
been doing so for ten years." [35]

Third, some other influences, of varying importance: *A
Voice from the Ranks: A Personal Narrative of the Crimean
Campaign by a Serjeant of the Royal Fusiliers* by Timothy
Gowing, edited by Kenneth Fenwick (1954); George Far-
quhar's *The Recruiting Officer*; John Whiting's play, *Saint's
Day* (1951); the American film, *The Raid* (1954); Rudyard
Kipling's short story, "Black Jack"; nineteenth-century army
ballads; Alfred Tennyson's "Maud"; and poems by A. E.
Housman.[36] Additional influences are Arden's observations
on the psychology of professional soldiers[37] and what he
called the "wish-fulfillment" element: "Many of us must at
some time have felt an overpowering urge to match some
particularly outrageous piece of violence with an even
greater and more outrageous retaliation" (7). Arden notes
that *Musgrave* was written rapidly and more intuitively than
most of his work: "The imagination was on fire when I
wrote the play but my intellect was somewhat in abey-
ance. . . . Really successful plays come out of a fusion of the
imagination and the intellect." [38]

Alan Brien astutely categorized *Musgrave* as melodrama:

The characters' reactions have always to be several sizes too large
for their actions. The mention of a man's name in a pub resounds
like a cannonade [26]. The drop of a trunk on a quayside starts off
tremors of an earthquake. The hoisting of a skeleton to a flagpole is
expected to change the world. Mr. Anderson [the director] accepts
the melodrama and even underlines and emphasises it in the style
of a UFA thriller [1920s German films]. He uses an eerie warbling
note like that of a musical saw to rivet our attention to the insanity
hovering above his characters. A sepulchral dissonant organ march
[by Dudley Moore] ushers in the acts. These are all, in a sense, Irv-
ingesque devices more fitting to the Lyceum than the Court.[39]

Brien correctly mentioned Irving: Arden read *Henry Irving: the Actor and His World* by Laurence Irving (1951), and saw Musgrave as the kind of role Irving played.

Onstage action and color are prominent in the play, Arden explains: "The first idea for the play came to me in stage terms partly because of its spectacle. I had seen a number of contemporary plays and felt—particularly with *Live Like Pigs*—well, this is all very nice, I like this play, but I can see, looking at it on stage, why some people don't like it. It *is* grey. And I suddenly wanted to write a play with a visual excitement as well as a verbal one. I visualized the stage full of scarlet uniforms." [40]

Scarlet in the play is the color not only of uniforms but of the mayor's gown, of blood, of playing-cards in the first and fourth scenes, of the "roses" used often to describe the soldiers. Two other colors are stressed, the black of the night, of colliers and collieries, and of Black Jack Musgrave's mind, and the white of snow and the skeleton. The several descriptions of the soldiers as "lobsters" brings two colors together, as lobsters are black and turn red when boiled!

Arden asks for only a few properties, "a selection from the details of everyday life . . . they should be thoroughly realistic" (7), so in performance the solid bar counter, the heavy trunks, and the rifles and Gatling gun are conspicuous. Stuart Hall praised especially the inn setting in the original production, "set in brown and blue, against a pale blue winter curtain; it has the strict severity of a Dutch painting, and takes up exactly the moral precision of Musgrave himself." [41] Arden conceived the play as a series of dramatic tableaux: the canal bank, the stable, the hoisting of the skeleton, the dance when the dragoons arrive.

Some of the language of the play is highly original, such as, "That serjeant squats in your gobs like an old wife stuck in a fireplace," (62); "Here's three redcoat ravers on their own kitchen hearthstone!" (92). David Rush praises the language as "rough, proletarian, frequently Northern in its rhythms, but at the same time highly-wrought and sometimes poetic. The effect aimed at often seems to be that of a strong but uneducated mind groping for words adequate to its thoughts. . . . Arden's technique of using working-class speech as a basic material, and then working it into an elaborate and poetic texture, is capable of almost infinite development." [42]

The play has more than twenty snatches of ballads, some of which appear to be traditional, while others show Arden's love of color and simplicity: "I am a proud coalowner / And in scarlet here I stand. / Who shall come or who shall go / Through all my coal-black land?" (15) There are also three major verse passages, for moments of "emotional pressure" [43] and "oracular pronouncements" [44]: Annie's conclusion on "for what a soldier's good," Musgrave's outcry while he dances, and Attercliffe's song referring obliquely to his wife and the greengrocer at the end of the play.

Theatrically, then, *Musgrave* is full of memorable language, of color and excitement. As important as its stage worthiness are its many ideas: the essential concept is the extreme difficulty of escaping from violence—at least in the world as presently structured. The picture is not simply of an impasse, however; *Musgrave* does more, showing problems within men and society (probably in any organized society, though there could be better leaders than the mayor and the parson). A solution may be for enough of the young to pursue life and love, as Sparky and Annie do, and for enough older people to view them with the understanding of Mrs. Hitchcock, especially, and Attercliffe. Simple kindnesses, like Mrs. Hitchcock's prison-visiting, are more effective than grand gestures on public platforms.

Chapter Four
Plays, 1960–63
The Happy Haven

The Happy Haven, written directly after *Musgrave,* has little resemblance to its predecessor; but Arden points out that the last scene of the later play is "practically the same" as the marketplace episode in *Musgrave,* "with the people pinned against the walls while an appalling act takes place in the middle of the stage." [1] *The Happy Haven,* which is intentionally experimental, was written while Arden was Fellow in Playwriting at Bristol University and intended for the University's Drama Studio, a converted squash court which seated one hundred and fifty. The play, first performed in Bristol in April, 1960, was subsequently presented, with the same director, William Gaskill, and some of the same cast in London at the Royal Court on September 14, 1960, for twenty-two performances.

"The Happy Haven" is the ironic name of an old people's home. Dr. Copperthwaite, who directs the institution, shows an inhuman, objective attitude to his patients. Copperthwaite, who perfects his discovery of "the Elixir of life—of Life, and of Youth," [2] plans to demonstrate its effects when the local mayor, a wealthy benefactor of the hospital, and a representative of the Ministry of Health, are paying a visit. At the same time the five patients' interests and way of life are shown: Golighty imagines that he loves Mrs. Phineus, and she cheats him in a game of hopscotch; Mrs. Letouzel schemes to obtain Mrs. Phineus's money; Hardrader keeps his dog hidden because pets are forbidden; Crape spies on the others for Copperthwaite and learns of the doctor's plans for them.

As the crucial day for the experiment approaches, the old people are given a brisk medical examination. When Crape fails the examination, he persuades the others that they would not really like to be rejuvenated, and Mrs. Letouzel finally perceives, "We don't want to die but we none of us dare state that we want any more life" (254).

The elixir is tested on the dog, who becomes a tiny puppy, and the old people succeed in stealing some of the elixir. In the final scene, and in the presence of the distinguished visitors, the inmates seize the doctor and inject him with some of the elixir. He becomes a small boy with a lollipop, and Mrs. Phineus takes him on her knee and sings a lullaby. The old people address the audience together in bland generalities—"Be cheerful in your old age. . . . Go home, and remember: your lives too, will have their termination" (272)—and Mrs. Phineus pushes the doctor off the stage in her wheelchair.

Arden's introductory Note states that "the play is intended to be given a formalized presentation" (193). Asked to define this statement more fully, Arden noted that he had in mind direct speaking to the audience, the dog (seen by all the characters, but not in fact present), and the use of music. In Dublin a pianist played throughout the production, as in silent movies. Most important for the effect Arden desired was "a permanent set, with a symmetrical lay-out, and not realist." Because he found the white and green flats used at the Royal Court "too clinical," [3] he used orange ones when he produced the piece in Dublin in 1964.

The most original device, however, was the use of masks. Arden instructs: "The Five Old People wear character masks of the *commedia dell'arte* type, covering the upper part of their faces only. The Doctor does not wear a mask, except at the very end, when he is shown in one that covers his whole face, and represents himself as a child. The Nurses and Orderlies have their mouths and noses covered by hospital antiseptic masks. The distinguished Visitors wear masks similar to those of the Old People, but less individualized" (193). Arden's interest in masks originated at the Royal Court's Writers' Group. William Gaskill, who was impressed with the results, commented that "the cast did achieve a breadth of style and a boldness of characterisation they could never have achieved in make-up, however grotesque.

The imagination *was* released by the mask, and for me absolutely justified the experiment."[4] The elderly, behind their masks, have a freedom of expression that, treated naturalistically, would be sentimental. The masks further the characters' humors: Mrs. Letouzel demonstrated greed; Hardrader, arrested youth; and Mrs. Phineus, frustrated motherhood. The masks also make the literal point that, for people, the public face, rather than any truer self, is the real thing.[5]

The masks also point to the parallels in Arden's mind to the *commedia dell'arte,* and to link the characters with the stock figures of the form is tempting: the Doctor with Harlequin, the intelligent rogue; Mrs. Phineus with Flaminio, the *ingenue*; Crape with Pulcinella, the intriguer; Hardrader with Capitano Spavente, the braggart; and Golighty with either Flavio, the juvenile lead, or Pantaloon, the unscrupulous merchant. Masks also emphasize humors more prominently than the other Jonson-influenced plays, *The Waters of Babylon* and *The Workhouse Donkey.* Arden to me remarked that "The concept of humors has validity for the comic actor, and most comedians still use it. Do you know Harry Worth [a British television comedian]? His humor is a man who's always getting in a muddle without knowing it." Arden also explained that the play began as a dream of a doctor attacked by his patients and forcibly fed with a drug. This fused with a one-act play by his wife (the piece should be titled "in collaboration with" her) about an old man and an old woman, which became the hopscotch scene.

The Happy Haven is something of a tour de force in its enthusiastic originality; for, apart from the masks, the initial attempt to use a particular arena stage, the blend of farce and traditional humor comedy, and the unusual subject and setting, there is much more inventive business. For example, the doctor tries to catch the dog with a plate of stew; the old man makes a seriocomic night raid on the laboratory to steal the elixir; and, in the scientific work, there is a kind of parody of the concentration on equipment in Brecht's *Galileo.*

Turning from technique to meaning, however, there is so much uncertainty that there are almost as many interpretations as there are critics.⁶ The two main themes, however, are Old Age and Science. These old people are childish and full of faults: jealous (Crape is unfit for rejuvenation, so he does not want the others to be); greedy (Mrs. Phineus eats Golighty's tea); unscrupulous (Mrs. Letouzel tries to steal Mrs. Phineus's money and Mrs. Phineus cheats at hopscotch); and, above all, pathetic (Hardrader's pride in his fitness, Mrs. Letouzel's repetitive reminiscences about enduring two world wars, Golighty's yearning for Mrs. Phineus). Except perhaps for Crape, these characters are admirable because they courageously face the truth and reject delusions about the past. And so for them rejuvenation is a punishment to be inflicted on Copperthwaite, rather than something desirable.

Like the Sawneys in *Live Like Pigs,* the old people are flawed, but Arden sympathizes with them. Mrs. Phineus's long speech states the message for all of them, "Leave me be, but don't leave me alone" (251). Clearly, too, the vices of the old spring partly from the way they are treated, snubbed by the nurses (as in 2.3) and given orders by loudspeakers. Mrs. Letouzel describes this dehumanization: "Here we are, look at us, dried up in this Institution, the only things we know how to do are the worst things we ever learned—plotting and planning, avarice and spite. Well, why not? We have no opportunity for anything different" (220). The visitors in the last act treat them as exhibits, and the satirical note in the play is strongest when the visitors make polite conversation that is heard as "wordless goggling noises which sound both patronizing and genial" (266). The attitudes of others toward old age are blamed much more than the people themselves.

The Happy Haven is equally about the dangers of Science; for, although Arden is not particularly penetrating on this theme, he is like many others in the humanities who see scientific advance as outrunning mankind's ability to control the discoveries. He raises the issues of the morality and consequences for individuals of new possibilities, such as heart transplants and kidney dialysis machines. Since this is a play, not a debate, Science is represented by one man, Copperthwaite. He calls himself Faust in the first scene (198); Crape is a Wagner in his parodying of his master's search and a kind

of Mephistopheles when he interrupts and ruins an experiment (200). Like Musgrave, Copperthwaite has singleness of
purpose and may see himself as God: Mrs. Letouzel calls him
"our Lord, Priest and Superintendent, great Guardian of the
Mysteries" (254). Certainly he is assuming the power of God.
He is the only one who wears no mask.[7] His up-to-date
science, ironically, pursues a medieval goal, the elixir of
youth. He is extending (or bending) the duty of all doctors to
preserve life to that of changing life. Two glimpses of Copperthwaite's life away from the Haven occur when he is talking on the telephone to his mother and to the captain of the
football team, and these moments emphasize his immaturity
in everything except research ability so that the concluding
act—his return to boyhood—is appropriate.

The Happy Haven remains hard to categorize, as the variety
of labels applied shows. Arden called the piece a "pantomime" first,[8] and later "a grotesque comedy."[9] Frederick
Lumley describes it as "sardonic farce,"[10] and Robert Hatch
finds it "dark fantasy, a cautionary fairy tale for adults."[11]
More farce than fantasy or comedy, *The Happy Haven,* like
The Waters of Babylon, amuses and surprises; and, like *Live
Like Pigs,* it leaves the audience with a new view of the
serious issues of old age and the role of science.

The Business of Good Government

The Business of Good Government is short, "a half-hour
play that took an hour when we performed it. We hadn't
allowed for the Somerset drawl."[12] In brief scenes, Mary and
Joseph come to the Bethlehem inn, the baby is born, angels
summon shepherds to visit them, the Wise Men visit Herod
and then Jesus. Joseph, Mary, and the baby flee to Egypt,
closely followed by Herod. At the frontier he questions a
farm girl who says, truthfully, that she was sowing the field
when the holy family passed, and that the corn is now
grown high. Arden knew of this apocryphal miracle because
the scene is depicted in a stained-glass window in King's College Chapel, Cambridge.

Most of the play follows the New Testament accounts. The
characters are convincing because Arden asked himself anew
how shepherds would react to an angel (one resents being

disturbed in the middle of the night) and how Herod would react to the Wise Men (he suspects they are on a government mission and so are keeping their real purpose secret). As the title suggests, Arden's particular interest is in Herod, the well-meaning administrator trying to maintain the independence of his small country.

The Business of Good Government was first performed at Christmas, 1960, in the village church at Brent Knoll, Somerset, where the Ardens were then living. Arden noticed that the church would be very suitable for a play, as the chancel was raised four feet higher than the nave, with no screen, so he visited the vicar and offered to write a play. Margaretta D'Arcy directed the production, and Arden played one of the Wise Men. This was the Ardens' first venture into writing for and working with a true community, which he has often sought since, as in the work at Beaford on *The Royal Pardon.*

The Workhouse Donkey

The Workhouse Donkey, which occupied much of Arden's time between 1961 and 1963, was commissioned for performance in the week of the opening of Coventry Cathedral in May, 1962; however, the Royal Court Company, which was to perform the play, found it unacceptable, even after revision; and Laurence Olivier eventually presented it at the Festival at Chichester, Sussex, which he organized in July, 1963.

The workhouse donkey is Alderman Butterthwaite, who was previously seen guiding Krank through the maze of local politics in *The Waters of Babylon.* Now Arden presents both Butterthwaite's earlier, glorious days as the power in an industrial town in the West Riding of Yorkshire, and his downfall there which led to his retreat to London. He is opposed by Sir Harold Sweetman, the local Conservative Party leader and a wealthy brewer. A new and incorruptible police chief comes to the town, Colonel Feng, an English gentleman who was formerly in the Colonial Service. Seeking to be impartial amid political and personal feuds, he soon discovers Labor leaders drinking after licensed hours, and also suspects a nightclub which is secretly financed by Sweetman. When

Butterthwaite is forced to rob the Town Hall safe, he is exposed—but Feng also has to resign. Other characters and plots revolve around Doctor Blomax, a Southerner, who announces "I am a corrupted individual: for every emperor needs to have his dark occult councillor: if you like, his fixer, his manipulator—me." [13] Blomax eventually marries Gloria, the manageress of Sweetman's nightclub who is made pregnant by Police Superintendent Wiper, and Blomax's daughter Wellesley is wooed both by Sweetman's son and by Colonel Feng. The lonely Feng's clumsy, abrupt, pathetic proposal is a fine scene with a different mood from the rest.

Arden subtitles this complex work "a vulgar melodrama," "to be understood in its original sense of a play with a musical accompaniment" (7). The first production used music during some dialogue, as well as settings for the songs, and between scenes. He associates this comedy with *Musgrave*: "The first scene is almost the same as the last scene in *Musgrave* as far as regards the characters on the stage and what is going on; you have again a public platform and the local authorities, the Mayor and Corporation and so on, getting up and making speeches; the atmosphere is completely different, but there is a definite attempt; when I wrote that first scene I did it deliberately, so that they almost link on from one play to the other." [14] A scene (1.3) in which a police constable closes a pub recalls the similar inn scene in *Musgrave*.

The main literary influence on the play is Ben Jonson, as Arden observed: "*The Workhouse Donkey* I would regard as a straightforward classical comedy in structure. It's based on the sort of Jonsonian type of comedy in which you get a fairly large cast, a contemporary theme with social comment in it and then an elaboration of plot which is not realistic but fantastic, ending up in a sort of classical shape to the play—you know, the various threads of the plot culminating in a big scene at the end, for instance, in which everybody's exposed, and the use of verse to give an extra dimension to the goings-on." Vaudeville conventions are introduced: "I'm also using some shreds from English music-hall and pantomime tradition, which are more apparent when the play's staged than when you read it." These two influences join at times, notably in Blomax, who is both a Jonsonian sly rogue and a vaudeville entertainer, twirling a stick and singing comic songs. Arden acknowledges a related inspiration, nineteenth-century theater: "the approach to the theatre, the type of staging, the strong lines of character drawing and plot that were involved, you know; they didn't go in much for subtle playmaking and I think that I'm very much influenced by that. I have one of these nineteenth-century toy theatres which I enjoy playing with." [15]

Bamber Gascoigne, writing in *The Observer,* could find nothing to admire in the Chichester performance:

Arden allows the most obvious stock types to dawdle through some very flaccid scenes and then tries to inject interest with a series of stylistic gimmicks. He borrows Brecht's device of characters breaking into blank verse when they say something pretentious. He genuflects to the early Joan Littlewood heresy that a play is somehow richer if every 10 minutes somebody breaks into a little chirpy dance. . . . None of this would matter—and some of it might even help—if only the drama behind the frills were solid, intelligent, gripping. . . . The gloomy fact is that the scandals of Arden's borough are extremely dull. I found it impossible to care how they would develop or who would implicate whom, and without this basic interest the gimmicks of style become pointless ornament. [16]

Other reviews were very favorable. Alan Seymour judged it "exactly the kind of play contemporary theatre needs," [17] and Philip French observes: "Why the piece hasn't been recognized as one of the half-dozen best British plays of the last decade is a mystery." [18] Charles Marowitz listed the virtues: "It is intelligent. There is a skill in the writing which breezily creates outsize characters and craftily develops a fanciful language to suit their dimensions. It is funny (not hilarious) and creates the sort of thoughtful laughter we expect from plays that do not set out to simply tickle our ribs. It is a generous play. It proliferates incidents; it tangles plot and sub-plot and, as it turns out, is generous to a fault. . . . It is meaningfully complex. Beneath a bouncy exterior lies a maze of meaning." [19]

The meaning is firstly the truthful portrayal of the urban

provincial way of life—with the lid off. To quote Arden: "I
wanted to set on the stage the politics, scandals, sex life, and
atmosphere of Barnsley, as I remember shocked Conservative elders talking about it in my youth. . . . Certain key incidents—the burglary at the town hall, the incident at the
Victoria, the politics of the art gallery, and so on—belong in
a not-so-veiled form to the politics of Barnsley." [20] Butterthwaite is described as "everybody's Uncle Charlie" and as
the Napoleon of the North, based on a Barnsley mayor who
liked to describe himself as Uncle Charlie, and on Joseph
Jones, a miners' union leader in the thirties and forties, who
was known as the "Napoleon of the North." The dismissal of
Chief Constable Popkess of Nottingham in July, 1959, and
the personality of Arden's father-in-law, a Dubliner who informed him on Irish politics (9), are also reflected in the
piece.

Arden insists that the play is true for places like Barnsley
which are "run by councillors who are mostly elderly men;
the Labour Parties are pretty conservative up there; they've
been based on a kind of Trade Union backing, and there's
also a pretty strong non-conformist attitude to life, and it's
all a sort of hangover from the nineteenth-century. I may
have exaggerated slightly for the purposes of the play, but I
don't think that I've given a false picture." [21] This remark
suggests a wider range of reference than is actually present:
there is little about the trade unions and nothing about any
of the churches—Nonconformist, Anglican, or Catholic.
The chief focus is on the inside of the Town Hall, which in
Live Like Pigs was a remote and mysterious institution,
manipulating the Sawneys and Jacksons. Arden reveals how
politics protect class interests with no thought of principle,
and how what happens in private is more important in
decision-making than public sessions (shown also through
Garnish in *Wet Fish*). Sweetman's home, with a maid to
serve drinks, contrasts with the public house where the
Labor leaders meet.

This public house is the "Victoria and Albert," and the
nineteenth-century name is one indication that Arden is also
alluding to the social history of the last two generations. Butterthwaite was born in a workhouse in 1897 and reveled in

the General Strike, when he was right to fight the police: "I remember the days in 1926 I'd ha' took twelve o'you blue-bottles on wi' nowt but me two boots and a twist o' barbed wire round me pick heft" (38). In the early thirties he was a hunger marcher:

> I marched in the hungry mutiny
> From the north to the metropolis,
> I carried the broken banner.
> When hungry bellies bore no bread,
> I dreamed of my dinner
> in the wasted line of dole. (96)

And he says, as Sir Hartley Shawcross said after Labor's 1945 election victory, "We're t'masters now" (19). While Arden is illustrating the old tag that power corrupts through Butter-thwaite and his local Labor Party, he shows too what has not changed: there are still rich and poor, and chief constables by training and temperament have more sympathy for the rich than for the poor.

The variety of language helps to convey continuity from a remoter past, as Albert Hunt indicates: "The play is full of broadsheet doggerel, music-hall ditties, songs that echo traditional ballads and there are sudden, startling moments when a few lines of verse reach the purity and simplicity of the best folk-poetry. . . . Their effect is to link organically modern society with the roots from which it has sprung. We are always aware of a present, different from, but shaped by the traditional experience of the past." [22] Arden remarked, too, that he sees councillors and industrial bosses as the nearest he can come in modern times to kings, the old subject of drama. [23]

The Workhouse Donkey is distinctively Northern, as *Live Like Pigs* and *Musgrave* are. The whole cast sings aggressively at the end:

> We stand all alone to the north of the Trent
> You leave us alone and we'll leave you alone
> We take no offence where none has been meant
> But you hit us with your fist, we'll bash *you* with a stone! (132)

Blomax in the opening speech declares that going north from

London involves "an appreciable mutation, (I mean, in land-
scape, climate, odours, voices, food)" (15). Accents, sets, and
the orchestra playing "On Ilkla Moor baht 'at" should convey
this Northern feeling in performance. Blomax continues:

> I put it to you that such a journey needs
> In the realm of morality an equal alteration.
> I mean, is there anything you really believe to be bad?
> If you come to the North you might well think it good. (15)

Morality, then, is relative, and the underlying theme is the
place of morality in the business of good government.

Feng is upright, too inhuman for ordinary mortals, while
Butterthwaite is corrupt, yet in Arden's view to be preferred:
"My view of Butterthwaite—this is a purely personal view—is
that the type of municipal corruption that he represents does a
great deal less harm to a community of people where it is
understood and lived with than the type of ferocious integrity
implied in the figure of the Chief Constable." [24] A rigid system
is incompatible with human energy and irrationality, qualities
Arden prefers to any absolutes. Only the mediocrities, the
Boococks and the Sweetmans, survive, together with the time-
serving villain, Blomax, who pursues his own advantage like
the Bargee in *Musgrave.*

Integrity—fortunately, in Arden's view—has limits: Feng is
trapped by his own repressed humanity when he falls in love
with Wellesley. He responds to trees ("They are a gentle entertainment provided by our Creator for ourselves and for Himself. It is churlish to abuse them," 80), and she significantly
works for the Forestry Commission and complains at the way
the park trees are trimmed: people, too, should be free, like un-
trimmed trees. This sympathy for anarchy is reflected in the
drama's loose construction; Arden in his Preface ideally sees
the play as continuing "six, or seven or thirteen hours."

This conclusion expressed in the figure of Butterthwaite is
the play's greatest strength. Arden sums up the character: "I
would find it impossible to see Butterthwaite as a character
in black and white. He seems to me, as I've written him, to
be a man who by the ordinary standards of political
behaviour obviously misconducts himself and yet on the

other hand he is a man of great capacity and vigour and spirit, which is more than can be said for most of the other people in the play." [25] He further "had a guiding ideal in his life when he was a young man, which still sticks with him in a curious fashion." [26] Mervyn Jones responds to the truth of the picture:

[Butterthwaite] is one of those Labour stalwarts in whom a rich relish for power and intrigue coexists with a stubborn loyalty to his class. He has long forgotten, if he ever knew, what he means by Socialism. . . . But he will never wear a dinner-jacket or modify his accent, anyone may call him Charlie, and his muddled ranting about the General Strike expresses a deep inner conviction. Whenever he pulls a fast one over the Tories, he glows with the delight of striking a lusty blow for the cause. I know Butterthwaite. I could not have been a reporter for *Tribune* without meeting him a dozen times. It is a measure of the class and regional limits of our theatre that he has never been put on the stage before; but here he is, and if Arden had done nothing else he would deserve our thanks for presenting Butterthwaite with total authenticity.[27]

Butterthwaite is more than a man Jones has known: he is an endlessly enjoyable mixture of rhetoric, cunning, stupidity, political concern, relish of life; he contains the contradictions of the Labor Party today; and, like the Sawneys and Johnnie Armstrong, he is a man who no longer fits into society.

Arden aims for "a raucous Aristophanic manner that would develop a poetic intensity," [28] embodied mainly in Butterthwaite. Poetic intensity is approached at the end of the second act as Butterthwaite sings and scatters money all around as he robs the safe, then fully realized in the final scene. The drunken Butterthwaite—who was born on Christmas Day—wraps himself in a white tablecloth, puts a crown of flowers on his head, and declaims like an Old Testament prophet:

In my rejection I have spoken to this people. I will rejoice despite them. I will divide Dewsbury and mete out the valley of Bradford; Pudsey is mine, Huddersfield is mine, Rotherham also is the strength of my head, Osset is my law-giver, Black Barnsley is my washpot, over Wakefield will I cast out my shoe, over Halifax will

I triumph. Who will bring me into the strong city, who will lead me into the boundaries of Leeds? Wilt not thou, oh my deceitful people, who has cast me off? And will not thou go forth with Charlie? (129–30)

Donkey references hint at Christ's entry into Jerusalem, and the crown at the Crown of Thorns before the Crucifixion. The date is the first of May, and Butterthwaite explains that this "is not only a day of Socialist congratulations but also a day of traditional debauchment in the base of a blossoming hedge-row" (118). Arden says he intended reference to the medieval Lords of Misrule,[29] with allusion also to ritual scapegoats, for Butterthwaite sings as the policemen take him away: "Out he goes the poor old donkey / Out he goes in rain and snow / For to make the house place whiter / Who will be the next to go?" (130)

The visual image unites pagan, Christian, and political images. In this final moment Arden arrives at Dionysian extravagance after his beginning in contemporary realism. This final episode, too, shows why *The Workhouse Donkey,* more than any other Arden play, demands to be seen. It is a virtuoso celebration: our lives are brighter because of a Butterthwaite, as well as for the pretty girls wearing bells and balloons in Sweetman's nightclub.

Ars Longa, Vita Brevis

Arden explained the origins of his short piece, *Ars Longa, Vita Brevis,* in an interview:

Having accepted, rather casually, a commission to write a piece for schoolchildren, I was at a complete loss until Margaretta D'Arcy reminded me of a curious inquest, reported in *The Times,* held on an art master shot in a wood while taking part in a Territorial Army exercise. Peter Brook then asked me for a little piece for his *Theatre of Cruelty* program, and we thought we would kill two birds with one stone. Miss D'Arcy had been doing some improvised plays with children in Kirbymoorside and also in Dublin, and she suggested that the peculiar directness and the spontaneous development of "classical" conventions which we saw in their work would be a useful starting-off point. *Ars Longa* is really more her play than mine—she decided what was to happen in each scene, and I then wrote down a sort of stream-of-consciousness dialogue to illustrate it. In order not to make the play too rigid for its potential juvenile cast—we weren't so worried about Peter Brook's adults—I did not attempt to polish or even revise this dialogue.[30]

Brook premiered the piece in a program at L.A.M.D.A. Theater in London on January 28, 1964.

Ars Longa begins with a private school headmaster's annual address to parents, a caricatured middle-aged conservative with the stock loyalties to police, authority, and the status quo. He appoints an Art Master, Antiochus Miltiades, apparently a man after his own heart, who does not believe in "free expression" and insists to his first class "no laxity, keep to purity of the forms, the line is rigid, the corners acute or obtuse or rectangular and everything sharp sharp sharp as the point of a bayonet." [31] But "rhythms" keep appearing in the pupils' work, and he lectures them on the value of military drill; within a few moments he is organizing them in a vigorous reenactment of the Battle of Camlann between Mordred and King Arthur. As he screams to them "Kill each other," the Headmaster intervenes and dismisses him. He returns home and orders his wife, Roxana, to bring him his tea at once, but she refuses.

Miltiades listens to a recruiting speech rather like Musgrave's and joins the Territorial Army, insisting that he wants as much discipline as possible, and goes with the soldiers into a forest, where they disguise themselves as trees as an exercise in camouflage. The Headmaster and the school Governors enter the woods to shoot deer, and the Headmaster deliberately kills the Art Master, pretending he mistook him for a deer. The Art Master's wife then "enjoys herself in fast cars with innumerable young men, all more handsome and less confused than her late husband" and the final words in the play are hers:

I shed a tear upon his bier
Because to me he was ever dear.
But I could not follow him in all his wishes
I prefer the quick easy swimming of the fishes
Which sport and play
In green water all day
And have not a straight line in the whole of their bodies. (20)

The fish of this image and the deer references associate with curves, movement, and spontaneous enjoyment as true art, contrasting with the rigidity of Authority, represented by the Headmaster's severe manner and the Art Master's insistence on straight lines, by soldiers marching and motionless as trees. But none of the three characters is associated crudely with only one side. The Headmaster is at first stuffy and pompous, not understanding youth and making only token concessions to independent thinking. When he sees that in the Art Master's hands discipline leads rapidly to chaos, he learns Authority is not the answer. While the Art Master's ideas on art may be ridiculous, Albert Hunt has pointed out that when the pupils misbehave behind his back in the classroom, "the man one would intellectually condemn is in fact made to suffer at the hands of the children whose side one would normally be on. It's very typical of the way, in Arden, the action cuts across and illuminates the words." [32] Perhaps, too, the Art Master's being is fulfilled in the few minutes of his marching with the Territorials. His wife has at the same time a genuine pity for him and a complete rejection of his beliefs.

The title invites speculation about the relations of art and life, as well as about freedom and authority. For the Art Master art and life are the rigors of army discipline, while for his wife both resemble the fishes swimming gracefully. Art and life cannot be bounded by discipline, and will flow free. Yet the exponent of authority, the Head, eliminates the enemy of true art, Miltiades. While at the end Roxana may carry art within her, art within a person is exactly as long or short as that person's life, a contradiction of *ars longa, vita brevis.* Possibly, too, art has somehow been realized in the Art Master's struggle to discipline himself.

Ars Longa is also about education, perhaps questioning whether art can be taught at all, or at least taught within normal school structuring. In this respect the play is well suited to performance by children, who will begin with an understanding of the scenes of the Headmaster's speech and the Art Master's lesson. Hunt explains that children's play was one of the inspirations for the piece:

One of the germs of *Ars Longa,* I understand, was a box of old clothes he and his wife got from a local junk yard. They put it in a shed outside their cottage at Kirbymoorside, and a group of local children came and dressed up and began to make their own plays. . . . What Arden is doing is taking some of the most simple facts of existence—such as that children like to dress up and pretend and tell stories and learn through pretending, and that we all, in fact, go on playing out roles for the benefit of other people—and he's using these simple facts to explore the most complex areas of contemporary experience. But everything starts in this excitement about playing. . . . There's this sense that using these theatrical materials is, in itself, an expression of freedom.[33]

Chapter Five
Three Historical Plays, 1963–65

Ironhand

Arden's three historical plays of 1963–65 are closely related, especially the first two, *Ironhand* and *Armstrong's Last Goodnight*. *Ironhand,* a free translation of Johann Goethe's *Götz Von Berlichingen,* was considered for production by the Royal Shakespeare Company but was eventually performed at the Bristol Old Vic in November, 1963. The play was televised in April, 1965, and was on radio in November, 1966.

Ironhand is Götz, who has lost his right hand in battle and replaced it with an iron gauntlet. He is a Free Knight, effectively independent and responsible only to a distant emperor: "I am a knight of hereditary status. I am a free feudatory of the Imperial power. . . . I am not the servile henchman of one of your Princes—I am the brother of the Emperor—look at my hand! Lost in *his* service—lost in *his* service, sirs." [1] Since the time is the early sixteenth century, higher authority can no longer tolerate Götz's robbery and violence. Götz first seizes Weislingen, emissary of the Bishop of Bamberg; and, after making an agreement with him that is soon broken, Götz robs a merchants' wagon-train. Besieged in his castle and forced to surrender, Götz is treacherously arrested and dramatically rescued during his trial. Blackmailed into leading a peasants' revolt, the rebels soon turn against him, and he is captured. Weislingen, the commander of the forces that violently suppressed the rising, plans to execute Götz but is persuaded to change his mind. Weislingen dies, poisoned; and, in the final scene, Götz is in prison, his legs in irons. He too dies, crushed; and his last speech expresses the conflict between freedom and order: "I stood by myself and I took no heed of nobody. All I said was freedom: All Weislingen said was some sort of order" (156). Maria, Götz's sister, speaks the final lines to Elisabeth, his wife, and also to the audience: "How can we talk about freedom and justice without accusing ourselves? . . . All that my brother said, and that he failed to do, is nevertheless possible. . . . Learn, Elisabeth, every day learn. You cannot afford not to" (157). Arden shows that freedom is desirable, but is incompatible with order.

While Herod and Feng represented incorruptible administration, Weislingen, who comes to believe that the end justifies the means, treacherously imprisons Götz after his surrender. He asserts: "There is terrifying anarchy enough in this Empire: I stand by the rule of law" (128). Like Musgrave, his singleness of mind grows dangerous: "We in our turn must therefore be possessed by a vision of Order, and we must allow no sacrifice to deter us from achieving it" (134). He ruthlessly suppresses the peasants, who fight under a banner inscribed "Naught but the Justice of God," a meaning of justice beyond his comprehension. Arden is again expressing not only his anxiety about total dedication to any absolutes but also his fear of authoritarianism.

Arden says the play appeals to him because of the inclusion of "such wide-ranging historical questions as the dispute between the partisans of the Roman and Common Laws, the Peasants' Revolt of 1525, and the ideas of the young Luther" (5) and "because it was written about a period of social change. The hero, Götz, is a romantic conservative, more than a bit out of touch with his times."[2] Almost every character notes that the times they are a-changing. Götz eloquently argues for the traditional ways: "I ride for what I always rode for and what my father rode and all our house before him . . . *I* say I am not afraid to be in error and to preserve that old injustice, if that is what it was, if by so doing I can also preserve the order of rank and hereditary truth that was given to us from the beginning, and which, rightly looked at, is the only framework of a life of freedom" (104, 105). When Weislingen tells him "those times are finished and done, Götz: they belong to a different age," he replies in a memorable phrase, "if they do, the pleasure and strength of life is falling from us all" (35).

The peasants fight, like Götz, for a return to traditional order, as one of their leaders explains: "We used to be free men in this part of Germany. . . . We had our own old laws, and all, to tell us we could do it. But the whole lot's been changed" (131). Whatever the horrors of violence in the Peasants' rising, the violence is direct and honest: Götz directs the rebels, "There is not to be one man killed except in fair battle" (132). But the new ways include the poisoning of Weislingen by his wife, her condemnation by a secret tribunal, and the hanging of Götz's squire (in Arden's version; in Goethe, the squire is killed in battle, a noteworthy change). The new diplomacy, which is usually Machiavellian, is bewildering for a simple, direct man like Götz.

Arden discovers in the early sixteenth century the time of change from the ordered and static world of feudalism and chivalry to a more complex and corrupt society. Exactly the same period is examined by Robert Bolt in his play about Sir Thomas More, *A Man for all Seasons* (1960); by Peter Shaffer in his play about the conquest of Peru, *The Royal Hunt of the Sun* (1964); and by John Osborne in *Luther* (1961), which also shows that the Peasants' Revolt was partially aroused by the spread of Luther's radical ideas (Luther himself appears briefly in *Ironhand*). Götz appears in another modern play, Jean-Paul Sartre's *Le Diable et le Bon Dieu* (1951), but the source is Cervantes's *El Rufian Dichoso*, not Goethe.[3]

While Sartre focuses on Götz's struggles to relate to God, such religious issues are mainly in the background in Arden's version. Götz is admirable in many ways; he keeps the loyalty of his wife, his squire, two Free Knights (Selbitz and Sickingen), and of his troops, who voluntarily choose to stay with him after his surrender. He claims to be a Robin Hood: "The men that I plunder are the gross merchant oppressors from the vampire cities that squat upon fields and vineyards" (37). He is exuberant: he likes living with danger, enjoying going to Nuremberg disguised to gather information. His troubles result from twice trusting Weislingen. Like Sailor Sawney and Butterthwaite, he is a larger-than-life individual for whom the modern world has no place.

Weislingen changes as time passes from the youthful companion of Götz and from the happy-go-lucky seducer with a lute to the butcher who signs one hundred and seven death warrants. As in *The Workhouse Donkey*, where the careers of Feng and Wiper are compromised by love, Arden suggests that private lives have much to do with public faces. Weislingen finds, when he tries to explain to Maria—his fiancée at the time—how he can love her while remaining loyal to the Bishop, that, "When I consider it, they do both mean the same. Politics and personality are all in a net together" (46). Weislingen's violence in later life is clearly linked, however, with his declining sexual satisfactions.

Arden's Introductory Note comments that "the vernacular vigour of the language is, I believe both new and truly wonderful"; and he adds that Sir Walter Scott in his translation could apparently not understand "the appeal of a play that treated of historical personages in vernacular prose, that varied that prose from the stately conversation of princes and emperors to the slang of soldiers and the regional dialect of peasants" (5). Arden is more successful with the dignified speeches of the churchmen and aristocrats, but the soldiers' grumbling—"Have you ever seen such a ramshackle bloody shambles as this night's bloody effort, eh? Soldiering? They call it *soldiering—I'd* call it the woodchoppers' harvest home, none but bloody mugginses invited, please come dressed as frogs and toads on account of the weather" (85–86)—is a passage not paralleled in Goethe's text.

Arden, in fact, describes his version as "a free paraphrase," but his later judgment is a critical one: "My version wasn't very good—too far from the original, yet not far enough to be a work in its own right."[4] Since Goethe's source was the autobiography of the historical Götz, most of his exploits in the play seem closely related to fact; but Götz's squire, Weislingen, Elisabeth, Maria, and Adelheid are all Goethe's creations. Arden's play is based on the 1773 version, the second of three, that is generally agreed to be the best. He worked mainly from the German, he frequently consulted also Scott's translation, and he notes four significant changes from the original: strengthening the role of Weislingen to make him a more worthy antagonist; tightening the structure; eliminating soliloquies; and making clear that Brother Martin is Luther. Arden nowhere acknowledges that Goethe did not design his play for performance, and he also appears to miss the fact that Goethe's primary interest was in the tragedy contained within Götz. Despite this, Arden writes language suited to the stage, as Scott and Charles Passage, the other recent translator of *Götz*,[5] do not. Arden's achievement is to make Goethe's first play more exciting and appealing to the present.

Armstrong's Last Goodnight

Arden's final comment on *Ironhand* is: "I have used it as a source for *Armstrong*, though, and a little for *Left-Handed Liberty*. So as a workshop piece it has served its purpose."[6] The parallels with *Armstrong* are indeed close, for they include not only the similarity between Iron hand and Strong arm, but also the same historical period; the same loose, episodic construction; the same conflict between the romantic conservative warrior and the unscrupulous modern diplomat. Scott is also a link, as Arden attributes the appeal of *Armstrong* to "the romanticism of border ballads, outlaws, and all the rest of what Walter Scott brought in."[7]

The conflict in *Armstrong's Last Goodnight* is between Johnnie Armstrong of Gilknockie, a semi-independent feudal chief on the western half of the Scottish Border, and Sir David Lindsay, ambassador for the young King James V of Scotland. The king needs peace with England, which is disturbed by the raids led by Armstrong. When Lindsay offers Armstrong the titles of Warden of Eskdale and Free Lieutenant if "he will follow the course of war ahint nae other banner than that of King James,"[8] Armstrong is delighted. To prove the king's good intentions, Lord Johnstone, the overlord of Armstrong's rival on the Scots' side of the Border, is imprisoned; but Armstrong's superior, Lord Maxwell, will not permit Armstrong his new title. Armstrong, who has in the meantime seduced Lindsay's mistress, is so furious when he hears the news that he rides off on another raid into England. When Lindsay visits Armstrong again, he finds him involved in a "religious orgasm" (105) aroused by a wandering Evangelist whose Lutheran ideas also interest Lindsay. McGlass, Lindsay's Highlander secretary, criticizes the Evangelist for sanctifying a man like Armstrong, and the Evangelist kills McGlass. When Lindsay goes to Armstrong for the third time, with a letter from the king as safe conduct, he invites him to join the royal party in a hunt. Armstrong is flattered and dresses in his richest robes. The king, who has had Lindsay as his tutor, meets Armstrong disguised, reveals himself, and then orders Armstrong hanged immediately from a tree—just as Armstrong has had a rival neighbor treacherously killed early in the play. Armstrong dies singing "But had I wist ere I cam frae hame / How thou unkind wadst be to me / I wad hae keepit the border side / In spite of all thy men and thee" (120). Lindsay delivers the final speech: "Here may ye read the varieties of dishonour, and determine in your mind how best ye can avoid whilk ane of them, and when. Remember: King James the Fift, though but seventeen years of age, did become ane adult man, and learnt to rule his kingdom. He had been weel instructit in the necessities of state by that poet that was his tutor" (122).

Of the various themes referred to in this speech, a minor one is that the king has "become ane adult man" by putting opportunism before principle for the first time. The point may be that the king has become like Lindsay, but, as the king has appeared in the play too little and too late, this theme is unrealized.

Much more important thematically is the mention of "the necessities of state," the requirements of order and good government. The means of achieving the necessities of state is negotiation, and the play is subtitled "an exercise in diplomacy." Diplomats are subject to complex pressures, and Arden comments about the play: "I've tried to present a situation in which everything is linked to another factor, until you can hardly get through the thicket at all. There is no simple answer, which is the natural situation in life. One is always coming up against circumstances in which one has to make certain compromises, which all seem right until they lead to others, and others—until one is completely turned about."[9]

In the play Lindsay is responsible to the king, who has to

bear in mind England and the Church's view, while Armstrong is responsible to Lord Maxwell, who is also responsible
to the king. The actual negotiators appears in the play—the
English Commissioners, not Henry VIII; the Political Secretary to the Cardinal of St. Andrews, not the Cardinal; the
secretaries of Lords Johnstone and Maxwell, not the peers
themselves. For Arden believes "these men are really responsible for the political decision of their masters, and know it"
(12). The National Theater program actually gives a chart of
the "power structure," in which the Church, the Court
(Lindsay), and the feudal lords and their vassals are all ranked
equally below the king.

Diplomacy, however, inevitably involves deception and
moral evil. Lindsay at first believes he can untie the Gordian
knot: "There was ane emperour, and he went with ane
sword and cut it. He thocht he was ane god, walken. Why in
God's Name could he no be a human man instead and sit
down and unravel it?" (28). But at the end, as Lindsay traps
the unsuspecting Armstrong, he puts on his herald's tabard
and says: "A like coat had on the Greekish Emperour / When
he rase up his brand like a butcher's cleaver: / There was the
knot and he did cut it" (112).

Just as Herod had to kill the children, Lindsay has to trick
Armstrong to his death. Lindsay is not the only dishonorable
one, for the final lines indicate also the theme of examining
"the varieties of dishonour." For the main characters are all
guilty in different ways: Armstrong has brought about the
death of a rival (Wamphray) as treacherously as his own
death is contrived, while Lindsay carries out the king's
policy and McGlass frequently advises Lindsay of the need to
use violence.

Edwin Morgan, writing in the theater magazine *Encore*,
argued that amid all these dishonorable acts, Arden made no
judgments: "It is a play about expediency, and it is expediency
of which the author does not visibly disapprove. . . . I find it
hard to exclude a feeling of uneasy disappointment—a feeling that I have been fobbed off with a theatrical pattern by a
man whose great talents should be devoted to exploring his
themes far more deeply and at a far warmer level of involvement. If Arden doesn't know what he thinks about kings and

outlaws, or gypsies and householders, or soldiers and colliers, or doctors and old women, he should *try to find out*. It matters!''[10] Morgan misses the passages in which Lindsay clearly condemns himself for his treachery. The dying McGlass advises him: "There is naething for you now but to match that same fury, and with reason and intelligence, sae that this time you will win," to which Lindsay replies sourly, "Will win and win damnation" (109). A little later Lindsay comments, "We are but back whaur we began" (112), which recalls Walsh's remark at the end of *Musgrave*, "We're back where we were," and Lindsay thinks his actions will be effective only for a year: "There will be nae war with England: this year. There will be but small turbulence upon the Border: this year" (121).[11]

Morgan's *Encore* review prompted Arden to write to explain his meaning:

I find the whole sequence of events in the play so alarming and hateful (while at the same time so typical of political activity at any period) that I have—perhaps rashly—taken for granted a similar feeling among the audience. . . . When I see a play about issues of moral importance, I very much dislike having their implications forcibly drawn to my attention. . . . Every play that tries to deal seriously with its subject must contain as many checks and balances as are compatible with normal theatrical length, if there is to be any degree of honesty in it. . . . My views on the Armstrong story are positive enough—Lindsay was wrong. But as to what he should have done to avoid self-destruction: there is a question that I cannot pretend to answer. . . . Lindsay's problem would not have arisen, at all, had he not subscribed to the belief in the necessity of government, and had he not undertaken to further this belief by serving the King. There is a basic contradiction between such service and the ideals of individual humanity that he expresses in my first act, and because he fails to detect this inconsistency, all his troubles come upon him.[12]

Arden's direct statement that "Lindsay was wrong" shows that the true subject is Lindsay's problems and changes in him. The balance of interest has changed from Arden's previous dramas: while in *Pigs* and *Donkey* one should be excited by the figures of Sailor Sawney and Butterthwaite (without wholly ignoring their failings), now their opponents' dilemma is central: the issues forced on an intelligent, humane man—and a writer too!—when he accepts a position of authority. Lindsay is full of paradoxes: lover *and* royal servant; poet *and* treacherous diplomat; potential heretic *and* king's tutor.

If Lindsay's end is, in Arden's word, self-destruction, this comes about for three reasons. He is too cerebral, lacking understanding of the emotional drives of a man like Armstrong, so that he is baffled when his mistress succumbs. Even after Armstrong's final raid, Sir David thinks of him as a man like himself and tells his secretary that Gilknockie "yearns in his mirk bowels, Sandy, for ane practicable rational alternative" (100). His approach to life, moreover, is insufficiently serious, being playful and overconfident: "I did ever tak pleasure in ane devious activity" (97). And, thirdly, he is a man of peace ("through my craft and my humanity / I will save the realm frae butchery" 27) who does not understand the nature of violence, any more than Musgrave did. McGlass bluntly tells him: "Ye did tak pride in your recognition of the fallibility of man. Recognize your ain, then, Lindsay: ye have ane certain weakness, ye can never accept the gravity of ane other man's violence. For you yourself hae never been grave in the hale of your life! . . . Your rationality and practicality has broke itself to pieces, because ye wad never muster the needful gravity" (108, 109).

Lindsay not only challenges Armstrong, he contrasts with him in many ways. On the literary level, as Arden points out, the Renaissance poet presents "a sophisticated Scots style as opposed to the rough style of the ballads."[13] Lindsay's mistress describes the difference, addressing Armstrong: "You are ane lovely lion to roar and leap, and sure wad rarely gratify all submissive ladies beneath the rampancy of your posture. You are indeed heraldic, sir. Emblazonit braid in flesh and blood, whereas David Lindsay can but do it with pen and pencil upon his slender parchment" (78). Lindsay can see both sides of Armstrong, that "he is ane potential magnificient ruler of his people" (100), and that his "purposes remain precisely the samen as ever they had been—violent, proud, and abominable selfish" (59).

Arden inevitably responds to Armstrong, commenting that

"to the ballad-makers of c. 1603 Johnnie Armstrong seemed 'the last of the giants,' and the song that was made of his hanging expresses this in clear 'Homeric' imagery."[14] Armstrong has admirable qualitities: he wants to be loyal, and says of himself: "They wad gain ane better service out of Armstrang gif they were to cease to demand it as ane service: and instead to request it—d'ye hear the word, request—to request it in humility as ane collaborate act of good friendship and fraternal warmth!" (80). Richard Gilman stresses that the man contains "an element of passionate life, a simplicity and directness which seen from a certain point of view puts the deviousness and calculated operations of the state to shame."[15] Yet he is sly, vain, uncouth, and impulsive, and at times childlike and even comic. He seeks power without responsibility, and when summoned by the king he dresses in "my gaudiest garments, ilk ane of them, a' the claiths of gowd and siller, silk apparel, satin" (114), and must look at least a little ridiculous. If there *are* heros in the play, they are not Armstrong or Lindsay, but, as in *Musgrave,* the women—Armstrong's wife and Lindsay's mistress.

Arden shows that the actions and attitudes of the two men must be considered within a broader social, political, and religious context. As elsewhere, sexual passion is opposed to cold reason and influences men's actions. Many of the songs and ballads refer to sex, at times sadly:

> The young men took me in their rankit line
> Ilk ane of them of a woman born.
> Till autumn cam in grief and pain
> And the leaves fell down across the lea:
> There was naething left for me to fulfil. (82)

more often happily: "Merry blooms the bracken bush / Whaur my true-love doth appear" (53). More direct references are various: McGlass says of Lindsay's mistress, "belike the lady will succeed whaur the politician fails" (83) in controlling Armstrong, and when the lady discusses him with Lindsay, she observes "in his ain een he is ane Emperour" and Lindsay retorts "aye, and in his ain codpiece, I daur weel hazard. For that's whaur it began" (94).

While Lindsay is willing to "postpone baith venery and poetry" (95), Armstrong indulges "wi' the lasses frae the tenant farms, or the tinker women upon the moss, or when he brenns ane house of the English" (74). Sleeping with Lindsay's mistress is Armstrong's first affair with a woman of his own class, and a consequence seems to be that he loses his stammer! That Lindsay openly has a mistress shocks Armstrong's wife, who asks her: "Amang the ladies of Edinboro and Linlithgow, are there mony like yoursel? . . . with nae reck of the vows of marriage—nae shame to be keepit mistress by a man that was weddit in kirk till ane other" (74), and tells her how a Border girl was punished for adultery. The difference between Edinburgh and Border attitudes is one of many facets of social change in the play.

As in the Germany of *Ironhand*, feudalism is declining and nationalism growing, and also the Reformation is about to reach Scotland. The Evangelist—though not fully integrated into the play—represents the individual free conscience and is like Armstrong in his urgent sexuality (though repressed), his impulsive violence (stabbing McGlass), and his ambition (for converts). Finally, Armstrong offers himself as an early Protestant martyr in his last speech by saying he is "the elect, the godly, me: washit white in the Blood of the lamb!" (119).

Arden admits he has made "rather free with the date of the Reformation" (8) in Scotland, which indicates that his interest is in the whole society and social situation of the time, as well as in a minor figure in Scotland's history. This interest is also shown in his direction on costume, which "should be 'working dress'—that is to say, each of the characters should be immediately recognizable as a member of his respective social class, rather than as a picturesque element in a colourful historical pageant" (10). The play frequently draws attention to the characters' costumes: in the second scene an English clerk observes: "My clothes express my function: unassuming, cleanly, subfusc," and he addresses Lindsay: "You, of necessity, wear your official livery, which is, of necessity, both splendid and delightful, and suited to the pageantry of state" (26). King Lear's "robes and furred gowns hide all" is recalled frequently: Lindsay puts on his scarlet robe of office before meeting the king, Armstrong is fascinated by the rich clothes in which Lindsay first visits him, the Evangelist criticizes the Lady's revealing gown, and Armstrong dresses and undresses on stage.

Arden suggests a permanent set, "within the medieval convention of 'simultaneous mansions,' " (9) with Armstrong's simple Castle on one side, and the royal Palace, "painted and gilded, and topped with pretty finials" (10), on the other, illustrating visually the primitive/civilized contrast. Between the two is the Forest, with many of the suggestions of mystery, fairy tale, sex, and religious orgy that forests have had from *A Midsummer Night's Dream* to Nathaniel Hawthorne's "Young Goodman Brown."

Critics found the language of the play difficult in performance: Ronald Bryden was "struggling headachily with the denser accents, as with rapid German,"[16] and Mervyn Jones's friends "frankly admitted that for them the play might as well have been in Japanese."[17] Such troubles are a matter of director's discretion—or indiscretion. The relevant questions are what is Arden trying to do, and does he succeed? Arden, as usual, explains himself in his General Notes:

It would clearly be silly to reconstruct the exact Scots speech of the period. . . . Scots was at this time a quite distinct dialect, if not a different language, and to write the play in "English" would be to lose the flavour of the age. The Scots employed by modern poets such as MacDiarmid and Goodsir Smith owes a great deal to Lindsay, Dunbar, Henryson and the other writers of the late Middle Ages and early Renaissance: but it is also a language for the expression of twentieth-century concepts. In the end I have put together a sort of Babylonish dialect that will, I hope, prove practical on the stage and will yet suggest the sixteenth-century. (8)

Arden, then, constructed, not imitated, a language. He used many features of present-day Scottish speech, like "wi' " for "with" and "mair" for "more," some archaic forms, of which "ane" as the indefinite article is the most conspicuous, and a relatively small number of obsolete words, like "burd" for "girl" and "corbie" for "crow." He fails only on the occasions when sixteenth-century terms come too close to twentieth-century educated speech, as in "He wad never swyve a lady. Haly Peter, it is inconceivable" (74).

Because the language conveys so well the place of the action and the sound of the period, William Gaskill, co-
director of the second production, said "Arden is to me a
writer a bit like Shakespeare in his approach, in that the
writing not only has to convey the communication, the
dialogue of characters speaking together, but also has to
carry the sense of the social environment, and the texture of
the people's lives; in addition it has to carry the writer's attitudes and his philosophies about the situation. All that has
to be supported by language. Now, what I think is marvellous about *Armstrong* is that Arden pulls this off."[18] John
Gross notes the mastery at the various social levels: "He is
particularly successful at catching a characteristically Scottish blend of bluntness and formality, the intimate and the
pedantic. His characters talk like lawyers at one moment,
peasants the next."[19] Undoubtedly to write such convincing
sixteenth-century Scots is a tour de force and creates a context in which ballads—and the primitive emotion, behavior,
and imagery of ballads—are appropriate.

Arden's inspiration is the Ballad of Johnnie Armstrong,
recorded by Francis J. Child in his *English and Scottish
Popular Ballads* in three substantially different versions, a
form of one of which is quoted in the National Theater
program.[20] The ballad describes the tricking and death of
Armstrong, which is the play's climax, though only one of
forty-two scenes. Arden's use of a ballad and its milieu is the
fullest example of his fulfilling the intentions of his 1960 article, "Telling a True Tale." Arden records that as he thought
about the ballad, "I was living in Ireland near a sixteenth-
century castle, and I began to imagine a *film* of the story
made in that particular location."[21] "But I soon had to drop
any idea of a cinematic treatment, because film-making in
this country imposes impossible restrictions."[22] The drama
has many brief and essentially visual episodes, however, suggesting that Arden wrote partly in terms of cinema, as
Penelope Gilliatt describes: "There is a clump-footed reel
that looks like a Brueghel, an almost cinematic shot of a girl
lugging the corpse of her untrue lover into the woods, a
hanged body that turns like a salmon on a hook, a ring of

soldiers with jagged black hair sitting in a Japanese-looking squat with one knee up and one on the ground. They are the sort of pictures that a child retains from narrative poetry read aloud.''[23]

Though the ballad records an actual historical event, probably of 1530, Arden reminds his audience that "this play is founded upon history: but it is not to be read as an accurate chronicle" (7). The historical Johnnie Armstrong was the most successful scourge of the Border, frequently leading raids into England. He controlled a large force and was protected by Lord Maxwell. Contemporary accounts vary on details, but in 1530 Armstrong was apparently tricked by the king, promptly hanged, and soon became semi-legendary.[24] Arden's major addition to the few known facts is to use Lindsay, author of *The Three Estates*, as the royal ambassador, but Arden points out that Lindsay was often sent on such missions, that his activities in the relevant year are not known, and that if he had been required to negotiate with Armstrong, he would have acted as he does in the drama.

Arden further is concerned with the universal issues of the deceits implicit in any exercises in diplomacy, as the other source—an unexpected one—shows: Conor Cruise O'Brien's account of his negotiations with Moise Tshombe in the Congo in 1961, *To Katanga and Back*.[25] While Arden says "I would not have it thought that I have in any way composed a *Roman à clef*" (8), he set out numerous parallels:

Tshombe of Katanga was a threat to the central government of the Congo if he remained a separatist leader. But he was not his own man. He was backed by Belgian mining interests and also by foreign governments whose activities at the United Nations bear a certain resemblance to the activities of Maxwell and his friends in Edinburgh. The attempt of the U.N. to persuade (and, finally, to force) him back under the control of the central government brought Dr O'Brien—a man of letters as well as a diplomat—into a society where intrigue (to which he was professionally accustomed) was no less common than violence in its most naked form. Who, for instance, killed Lumumba? Did Dag Hammarsjkold's aircraft fall out of the sky on its own, or was it induced to fall, and if so, by whom? The fact that a man like Dr O'Brien found himself immediately confronted by such apparently melodramatic questions which urgently required a realistic answer suggested to me the introduction of Sir David Lindsay into the play. The play is dedicated to Dr O'Brien, but Lindsay does not *represent* him, as Gilnockie does not represent Tshombe nor Wamphray Lumumba.[26]

The idea of Edinburgh as the focus of wider political activity is comparable, as it were, to the idea of Pan African unity.[27]

Armstrong will be a character rather like some of these African politicians. There's a type of man at present in these new countries in Africa who seems to have this curious combination of practical ruthlessness with almost hysterical emotion, which you don't find in European politicians much these days but which certainly you did in the sixteenth-century. I mean a man like Lumumba who was commonly represented in the Western Press as being almost a certifiable lunatic in fact would have got on perfectly well with the people at the time of the Wars of the Roses. You know, they would have understood this bursting into tears in public speeches.[28]

Arden appears to be protesting too much and trying too hard in some of these parallels. If he had not told us, we would not see the 1961 Congo events in his drama. These statements show his wish to relate past and present, finding African leaders more comprehensible in terms of medieval England, and the essence of diplomacy unchanged from period to period and from continent to continent. They reveal, too, that he is very anxious to relate his art to his political interests, to justify his play as—among other things—a political lesson.

Armstrong's Last Goodnight was first performed by Glasgow Citizens' Theater in May, 1964. Apart from the value of a Scots cast, Arden wanted the actor-manager of the theater, Iain Cuthbertson, to play Armstrong after seeing him play Musgrave the previous year. The second production was at Chichester Festival in July, 1965, where *The Workhouse Donkey* had been acted two years earlier. The co-directors were John Dexter and William Gaskill, who had directed *The Happy Haven* at the Royal Court, and the excellent cast included Albert Finney as Armstrong and Robert Stephens as Lindsay. The production transferred to the National Theater in October. The Theater Company of Boston gave the American première on December 1, 1966.

Yet again the critical reception was mixed. Bamber Gascoigne wrote that "the final effect is of many truths being stated and none being investigated,"[29] and Harold Hobson found it "a ragbag of clichés old and new. . . . In the end the sheer, intolerable boredom is too much for one's strength. Last Tuesday at Chichester was a penal experience."[30] Ronald Bryden, on the other hand, was excited: "Besides the spry diagrams we accept as plays in London, Arden's is a tumultuous oil painting."[31] Tom Milne concluded: "Arden's play—language, emotions, situations—is as rich and full-blooded as anything seen on the English stage for years, and miraculously it has received a performance to match."[32]

While the play is rich, it is less rich than *Musgrave*. There are similar situations—a girl crazed by the killings of her lover; a man abruptly killed with his own dagger, precipitating the death of another—which are both the misfortunes of individuals and the timeless subject of a hundred ballads. While in *Musgrave* they are embodied in the main plot, in *Armstrong* one searches for reasons and motivations. *Armstrong*, however, is rich in paradoxes: preconceptions about what happens when civilized diplomat meets primitive rebel are shaken, as the faults on both sides emerges; liberal assumptions about wise O'Brien against bad Tshombe are not borne out; the hanging of the man in the title role is not the tragedy that might be expected.

Armstrong was revived at the Northcott Theater, Exeter, in Fall, 1973, in a revised text, shorter and with simpler language. The rewriting was done initially by John Dove and Rhys McConnochie. The latter told me: "Arden was very helpful. We sent him the first draft of the cuts and he sent it back with his approval and several modifications. Arden, at our request, rewrote the beginning of Act 3, moving the action along faster while retaining the lyric quality of the scene. He also rewrote several speeches but the individual words and phrases translated into modern language were ours, sometimes rather clumsily, I think." The largest change in this new version that is clearly Arden's, then, is summarizing the first three scenes of act 3 in a monologue by Lindsay.

The following clarifications are probably Arden's work. The dialogue about Henry VIII and Lutheranism (69) becomes:

Cardinal's Secretary:	My maister the Cardinal of St Andrews looks with grief upon the wark of King Henry Tudor of England. Defiance of our haly Father the Pape and exaltation of rank heresy within the boundaries of that land! Whilk boundary is now protectit by the man that this Lindsay put there . . . his servant, gif ye will—Armstrong, the leal friend of the traducer of the Kirk.
Lord Johnstone's Secretary:	D'ye mean the entire business is ane heretical Lutheran plot?
Cardinal's Secretary:	Gif ye will, sir, gif ye will—it's no yet come up for judgement: but the provisional opinion of the Cardinal wad dam the hale thing, utterly. We maun rescue our sovereign Lord King James form six perilous possibilities. Under nae circumstance whatever maun the King be permittit tae give scandal to the faithful.

Lindsay's expectations and his instructions to McGlass on the messages he is to take to Armstrong (82–83) are also stated much more explicitly:

McGlass:	Will the King arrest Maxwell?
Lindsay:	(shakes his head) He is still free and in the pay of the English. So he will try to persuade Armstrang to raid across the border and start a war. I maun stay to prevent him. Ye maun gang on your own to Eskdale.
McGlass:	Can we offer Armstrang a certain Lieutenancy? He'll turn to Maxwell otherwise.

Lindsay: Na, There's no firm offer. Tell him I'm still
           working on it. Talk with tact, Sandy, play for
           time. Forget ye are an Heilandman. Above all
           we must not let him raid . . . God gang with
           ye.

The cuts, it seems, are merely approved by Arden. They include deleting three of the Evangelist's five scenes (1.8; 2.1;
3.7). His motivation to stab McGlass (107) is made stronger
by the latter challenging him with "It wad be better to
deliver up this Evangelist to the fires of the Cardinal, as
prescribit in the law," and then pushing him off his
preacher's box. The episode of the first letter from king to
Armstrong (49–50) is omitted, and three scenes in act 2 (11,
12, and 15) are substantially cut. Various exchanges, such as
those on pages 66–67 and 86–87, are abbreviated. Many of
the longer speeches are reduced in length, as are, more regrettably, some of the passages of verse and song (the first
half of Lindsay's, 26; the first half of Meg's, 37; the second
half of the Lady's, 81; the second stanza of the Maid's song,
82).
     Most of the unfamiliar Scottish words are changed "Usque-
baugh" (30) becomes "whiskey"; "sackless" (35) "helpless";
"forbye" (48) "moreover"; "nolt" (49) "cattle"; "creish"
(50) "fat"; "sark" (50) "shirt"; "gey" (73) "very"; "yetts"
(75) "gates"; and "Ersemen" (118) "highlanders." Various
proper names are eliminated, among them Gogmagog, Cy-
clops, and Gallowglass (59, 108); the quotation from Virgil
(113) and nearly all the Gaelic sentences are given only in
English. The new text appears markedly an improvement
from the viewpoint of audiences—at least outside Scotland.

Left-Handed Liberty

Left-Handed Liberty, which was commissioned by the
Corporation of the City of London to commemorate the
750th anniversary of the sealing of Magna Carta, was first
performed at the Mermaid Theater in June, 1965; and Boston
Theater Company gave the American première in January,
1968. Arden, who had nine or ten months in which to write
the play, explains: "I did not accept the job until I had

studied a bit, and then, although the story did not seem
naturally to lend itself to dramatic form, I found myself sufficiently interested to carry on."[33] The books he studied, the
main sources of the play, were *King John* by W. L. Warren
(1961) and *Magna Carta: A Commentary* by William Sharp
McKechnie (1905, revised 1914). Presumbably because of
the limited time available for its writing, the play includes
issues that are resolved clumsily or not at all.[34] Although
Arden told an interviewer that the final version (the prompt
copy at the theater) differed substantially from the published
text, [35] the prompt copy, apart from substantial deletions,
shows only scene 7 of act 3 as much altered. Arden expands
the 1965 references (that is, that there is still one law for the
rich and another for the poor), notably John's conclusion:
"Magna Carta, woe unto you when all men speak well of
you!"

By having the Charter sealed in the first act, Arden characteristically makes an unexpected approach to his subject. The
sealing is preceded by this striking scene: "A dark stage, two
pools of light. In one, a golden diagram of the Ptolemaic
circles, emblems of order, government and cohesion. In the
other, Pandulph the Papal legate, addressing to us a homily
about the state of the world. He tells us, directly and calmly,
that nothing has really happended since the Crucifixion,
nothing can happen until the Second Coming. We are sucked
into the time, the flavor and perspective of the thirteenth-
century, effortlessly. Arden puts us right inside the medieval
world at one bold stroke."[36] Then, "a queen snaps into
view, sitting on a high throne, rigid with age and about to
die, with 10 feet of robes and furs pouring down to the floor
like guttering wax; she mutters some incomprehensible personal history and is removed suddenly backwards, throne
and all. Liberated by his mother's death, a tub-shaped King
John with a choleric sense of humor starts to swoop over the
stage as though England were the chessboard in *Alice*."[37]

In the sealing ceremony that follows, John keeps the
barons guessing up to the last moment whether or not he
will accept the agreement. The barons' leaders are Fitz-
walter, who places his trust in force ("His soldiers are in
Flanders. Mine are across the river" [20]),[38] and De Vesci,

who worries about the wording of the treaty ("There is too much latitude in the Charter. I am highly suspicious of it" [47]). When the Marshal and the Archbishop are introduced, both are torn between their duties to king, barons, country, and Church. In a lengthy Council that follows, debates occur about stopping John recruiting foreign mercenaries and about who shall garrison the Tower of London. The next scene—one enlivened with dance, song, and a perfunctory game of dice—shows the barons with their whores, together with Lady De Vesci and the Mayor of London; and it is succeeded by a whimsical scene in which the king dispenses justice. Six more scenes report the events of the civil war, which resumed two months after the agreement at Runnymede, and include a glimpse of the King of France. Then the house lights are switched on, John takes on a 1965 existence with a speech of justification and explanation, and finally drowns when attempting a dangerous shortcut at low tide, an episode that uses mime, verse, and prose summary.

Magna Carta is first seen in the play as ostensibly a peace treaty between king and barons with many admirable guarantees of liberty that were intended by the barons to give them more power. The barons greedily want to remain armed against the king as well as to have the benefits of the Charter. The king, who knows their desire, signs to gain time; and neither group acts in good faith. Gradually it emerges that John, who has to some extent anticipated the genuine influence of the document, has subtly worded some clauses so that they promote liberty and restrict unscrupulous actions by both sides. While nobody at the time grasped the Charter's full meaning, the king shrewdly realized the value and the consequences of the ambivalence, or ambidextrousness, of the wording. The king shows another kind of ambidextrousness; he does not let his left hand know what his right is doing, so that the recruiting of mercenaries goes on even as the possible use of the Charter is first glimpsed by Lady De Vesci and the Archbishop. Men are too complex, moreover, to accord with absolute values like the liberty written about in treaties: men will always put "kinks" into the perfect Ptolemaic circles (8, 12, 85). The play's major statement is no doubt a new view of both John and Magna

Carta for most readers. Yet this idea does not make a play—or even an essay. Instead, largely detached from this thesis about Magna Carta, the play *refers* to varied events, gives an enjoyable picture of King John, and presents innumerable glimpses or passing references to other issues or facets of life.

Arden mentioned two of the other issues that arise by describing the subject as "the feudal system beginning to crumble,"[39] but V. S. Pritchett expresses this aspect more forecefully: *Liberty* is "about a historical break in men's minds."[40] But of course the Renaissance did not begin in 1215, and Arden is presenting the Charter as one stage in the changing balance of power between king and people and not as the crucial turning point. The crumbling of feudalism is central in both *Ironhand* and *Armstrong*. Another recurring theme is the complexity of responsibilities borne by men in public life: the barons look to France and even to Scotland, and the Archbishop is responsible to the Pope as well as to John.

The piece is set, Arden adds, "in a framework of medieval theology and cosmology."[41] "Framework" may be taken literally: Christ's Second Coming and Pharaoh's drowning in the Red Sea are mentioned at the beginning and end of the play, and the latter is even paralleled by John's own drowning. This act is the theological answer to John's account of humanity on earth: when John charges Pandulph, "Have you no answer to my tortuous eloquence?", he eventually replies, "Thou fool, this night thy soul shall be required of thee" (92).

While the two churchmen and their world view are prominent, they are only one of the several levels of society that appear, somewhat schematically. The Mayor of London—a more dignified mayor than those in *Musgrave*, *The Happy Haven*, and *The Workhouse Donkey*—appears to delight the Corporation who gave the commission but also because "this was the first time that the commercial middle class took an active part in English politics" (xii). While John meditates about the baffling nature of financial problems (75), economic issues are not resolved or explained. The common people are represented by three whores and by the three figures who seek justice from John: a foolish goldsmith, his wife, and a mandolin-playing priest—a group that prompts a condescending view of the masses. Act 3, scene 5, presents seriously the effect of events on the commoners, the demoralizing effect of the war, and their discovering that they too can interpret Magna Carta to their advantage.

The whores and the girl who deserted her husband for the priest also contribute to a group of hints about the status of women, Courtly Love, and the influence of sex on public behavior, another theme explored more fully in *Ironhand* and *Armstrong*. In the first scene Queen Eleanor recalls youthful amorous intrigues: "Sometimes for my lover / Sometimes for my poet / Always I kept the back door unlocked / Never for the King" (6–7). Later scenes show adulterous relationships between John and Lady De Vesci and the Young Marshal's idolization of her, so Arden is showing varieties of love from the prostitutional to the unattainable ideal in feudal society. Arden shows, too, that such relationships are affected by the Charter: Lady De Vesci cites it to justify her defiance of her husband, and John quotes the clause relieving women of the right to require men to duel on their behalf as a sign that "the Age of Chivalry is dead—1215" (85). Yet essentially what is seen of women in the play has, in Pritchett's words, "an intended importance which Mr. Arden has not rescued dramatically from some essay he has in mind on the end of the Middle Ages and the cultural dilemma of chivalry."[42] Arden intends, therefore, to present a picture of an age, as well as of John, and to document and dramatize part of the story of Magna Carta.

While *Left-Handed Liberty* presents a new look at constitutional history and overflows with comments about treaties, women, liberty, and so on, these ideas are often not incorporated into the play. Instead, discussion is lengthy and stage action conspicuously lacking. Such distinction as the play has is found in the figure of King John. Arden acknowledges that "perhaps I view his character and motives too favorably. It is difficult, however, to resist the rather weird charm of any of the Plantagenets when one comes to examine their personalities at close range" (xi). John's affinities are with the devious trio in the earlier plays, Krank, Butterthwaite, and the Scottish soldier. Like them, he is greedy, impulsive, cunning, clownish, skeptical, and is doing more good than harm. John is neither a hero nor the bad king of most history books; he is a rich addition to Arden's gallery.

Chapter Six
Plays, 1966–68
Friday's Hiding and *The Royal Pardon*

When *Left-Handed Liberty* was succeeded by another com-missioned work, Arden produced a far slighter one, *Friday's Hiding*. The commission was for a mime, and Arden and his wife together devised what they subtitle "an experiment in the laconic." The story is about a mean Scottish farmer who is so reluctant to pay his two hired men that every Friday afternoon produces a seriocomic situation in which he hides while the laborers scheme to wheedle the money from him. The action includes the men's thinking they have killed the farmer, his sister's taking the cashbox key, and the sister's possibly marrying one of the employees. Arden notes that "it is intended (beneath its farcical surface) to be an accurate representation of certain features of modern country life. . . . The play in sum is an ironic statement—*not* an affirmation—of the deep rootedness of conservative values."[1] The piece opens and closes with songs and there are a few spoken lines. Even with these aids, the "experiment" is elaborate for mime, but the laborers at work are suited to the form. When *Friday's Hiding* was performed at the Royal Lyceum Theater, Edinburgh, in March, 1966, the Ardens hoped to be present during rehearsals to test the value of their ideas; but, since they were unable to go to Edinburgh, they had no op-portunity to learn more about the techniques of mime.

The Royal Pardon, which is subtitled *The Soldier Who Became an Actor*, is written for children. In a past described as "legendary rather than historical," a group of strolling ac-tors perform a short verse play about St. George and the Dragon. Arden told me he saw the troupe as "a cross be-tween the *Hamlet* players and the *Nicholas Nickleby* players." The actors are chased out of town for indecency by two Keystone Kops policemen, but soon reappear, waving a Royal Pardon, for all theatrical troupes are summoned to perform before the king. The police, meanwhile, have arrested for vagrancy a soldier just returned from a war. The soldier quickly escapes by knocking out the constable, and finds the actors rehearsing "King Arthur" for performance at court. He repairs their scenery and is allowed to join them. The players so impress the court that they are sent to France to appear at the marriage of the English prince and the French princess and to compete for a prize against a French company. The constable, who has followed the soldier by a trail of crumbs, rows in his pursuit in a small boat. Because most of the English players are ill, their play is two "real" events: the soldier fights the constable and also falls in love with the young actress Esmeralda. Finally, the constable is turned to stone, the English group judged the winners and appointed as court players; and the soldier and Esmeralda will marry and, together, "entertain the people."

The Royal Pardon was written for the opening of the Beaford Arts Center, in Devon, and first performed there in September, 1966. Arden and his wife directed; Arden himself played the constable with a largely student cast. The hall at Beaford, which measures only twenty feet by thirty feet, accommodated ninety people; it had no raised stage; and its two doors were used by cast and spectators. But, to the Ardens, "these conditions were not a handicap to be overcome, as we had hoped and indeed planned for them from the beginning."[2] It played at the Arts Theater, London, at Christmas, 1967, and again at Easter, 1968. Although the piece was advertised at the Arts as intended for children of eleven years and upwards, the authors' comment that it originated "in a series of bedtime stories told to our own children (aged 2–6): but we intended the dramatized version to be for a somewhat older age group. The production in Devon, however, seemed to suggest that there is sufficient in the plot and action to interest even little children" (7).

The story is easy to follow and full of incident. Costumes can be varied and colorful, and the jokes are numerous: "Do we look like assassins?" "You would be very poor assassins indeed if you did" (63). "Are you by chance a Democrat?"

"No, I'm not, I'm a perfectly respectable professional" (68–69). Above all, there is plenty of vigorous comedy: St. George kills the dragon with "a good deal of business," the soldier breaks out of prison with an enormous file, a trellis keeps falling in the "King Arthur" rehearsal, a shipwreck is mimed by the actors, the constable can't reach his truncheon when disguised; but most of these comic moments are in the first half.

The serious content is the "let's pretend" of the young child, the glamor of theater contrasted with the outside world for the older child, and illusion versus reality for their parents. The actors sing of this paradox at the start: "All is painted, all is cardboard / Set it up and fly it away / The truest word is the greatest falsehood, / Yet all is true and all in Play" (11). The focus on plays and actors permits many variants on drama as illusion imitating reality. Actors are masked for both their plays, the soldier wears the clown's mask and later a false nose to evade the constable while the latter appears disguised both as a Beefeater and as a French officer. There is a rehearsal and a play within the play, and the final conflict between the soldier and the constable is real for them but part of a play for the onstage audience, while the theater audience perceives both of these and knows that they all are "really" actors. *The Royal Pardon* is, such an original and enterprising venture into a new field that one regrets that the Ardens have not written for children again.

"Harold Muggins"

Late in 1967 Arden and Margaretta D'Arcy began working with Cartoon Archetypical Slogan Theater, an agitprop group presenting improvised satirical shows, because the Ardens found they shared political attitudes. Arden observed of the method: "You might say it's like *commedia dell'arte*, improvised round a set theme."[3] The result of this collaboration, "Harold Muggins Is a Martyr," was staged at the old-established, leftwing, semiprofessional Unity Theater in North London in June, 1968. Arden and the group sought to interest and involve the whole community.

As a result of this intention, street parades and shows, in

the style of the New York Bread and Puppet Theater, were
held, as were meetings on local issues at Unity. Performances
were preceded by a carnival outside: "On the garden walls of
Mornington Street a line of children balance and shout. In
the front yard of the little Unity Theatre, the playwright's
wife, in a fancy wig, banged a drum; the playwright's
children sang giggling parodies of TV adverts and the
playwright himself, in false moustache and seedy silk hat,
barked at you to roll up."[4] The carnival included speeches
for and against the condemnation of Muggins. The environment, which was created inside and outside the theater by
art students, consisted of enormous examples of garish bits
of commercialism, such as a huge ketchup bottle with the
contents slowly oozing out.

The piece itself, advertised in advance as a "Gala/Festival/
Play/Celebration/Hit" and in fourteen scenes, showed Muggins and his wife, played by the Ardens, as operating a small
and struggling café. They deal not only in pornography and
prostitution but in receiving stolen goods. But their
customers change from them to the new supermarket which
has its "trained staff selected for your pleasure by scientized
sanitized computer personnel selection networks." Further-
more, Mrs. Muggins has threatened to throw out the Public
Health inspector, leading to court cases.

Grumblegut, a businessman, and Jasper, an accountant,
propose to take over the business, and the former offers explicit social comment: "The man that gives you green shield
stamps / Puts both your wrists in iron clamps. / The engineer
who builds a car park in your street / Is pouring liquid concrete round your feet." Once an agreement is signed with a
dubious lawyer, painters and shopfitters swarm in to give a
modern look to the store by installing Muzak and fruit-
machines and by renaming it "The Subliminal Experience."
Mrs. Muggins, unhappy at the changes, asks to see the top
man and is told by the Clerk of Works: "Supposing we was
to tell you that there simply isn't a head man? Suppose we
was to tell you that we are all controlled by the progressive
will and demands of the unrestricted flow of freedom." But
Grumblegut says a Mr. Big exists.

The new look increases the number of customers, but they

fight, cause damage, and assault the Mugginses. His three loyal employees ask for higher pay; and, when the new-look Muggins refuses, they leave. When Grumblegut and Jasper reveal "the Organization" will be deducting protection money and taking thirty percent of the profits, Muggins eloquently defends his acceptance of the changes: "Some of us, thank heavens, are not just sitting and yelling slogans, but we're making a definite effort to inject a bit of liberalism where it has the most effect, like in the apparent seats of power—the top of the Organization. The only way to work effectively is to work within the existing system: and I am passionately convinced of that." Mrs. Muggins disagrees, and decides to resist: "As from this moment a new Mrs. Muggins is born / The gunbelt with its lethal cartridges which before she has never worn / Is now with a calm clean gesture picked up from the dusty floor / She girds it round her vivid hips and strides towards the door." So she sets out to recruit a local gang to fight back.

The Organization sends a stripper, "three waitress/hostess/chorus-girl/tarts," "a head-waiter type, heaps of poofery," and "one of them horrible sergeant-blokes what stand at the door in a top-hat and all the gear," and they are threatened into staying. Finally, the local gang, disguised as customers, beats Jasper and drives out Grumblegut; and it then announces that in future its members will protect the café. They seize the girls and an orgy begins, but it is interrupted by the return of Grumblegut and his gang. "Terrible mayhem," states the stage direction, "Nobody left apparently alive at the end of it except for the Muggins and Grumblegut." And the latter has the last word: all can be repaired quite easily, but a report and investigation are needed. Then an actor (a different one each night) steps forward to seek audience reactions.

Arden explained: "It's really about how [Muggins] gets into his situation. The play doesn't give a verdict on him, it's not a directly didactic play. We're not saying 'look, the guilty man'; the verdict is implied."[5] D. A. N. Jones defined Arden's attitudes as combining "a ghostly Border Ballad appreciation of original sin with an annoyed, informed, wholemeal-bread criticism of TV, plastic and psychedelic cant,"[6] and Bryden suggested the play was "a British equivalent of Brecht's *Arturo Ui.* Instead of a gangster, his anti-hero is a gangster's fall guy." The critical reception was mainly hostile; Bryden even described it as "surely the stupidest play ever written by an intelligent writer."[7] Whatever the shortcomings of the play, the atmosphere of collaboration and social-political purpose in art and in the community was exciting, and Trussler found the scene "reminiscent of Theatre Workshop's early unrecognised days at Stratford East."[8]

Squire Jonathan

A few days after the opening of *Harold Muggins*, another play, *The True History of Squire Jonathan and His Unfortunate Treasure* (written five years earlier, in 1963), was presented by a group known as Inter-Action/Theatrescope Original Lunch-Hour Theater Club, once again outside the theater district of London, at the Ambiance Restaurant in Queensway.

The setting was a room with a large harp, a wooden chest, a brass horn which also served as a telescope, a fire, and a stool. A low white wall suggesting battlements surrounds the room, and a toy drawbridge is on one side. Outside the castle is grass and a pool of muddy water. Squatting by the fire is a little man, with long lank red hair, faded velvet doublet and hose; a huge key in his belt, he soon tells us, unlocks the chest which is full of jewels. This chest consoles him for his loneliness and unfulfilled plans, for it, "known alone to me, / Lives in its quiet life my true / Inherited treasure, and my love."[9] The man is Jonathan, who describes his fear of the Dark Men outside who "walk with a curious stiffness as though upon stilts" (22). He yearns for a "mountain of a white woman," for "without such a woman all this treasure is worthless" (23). At last, such a woman arrives, having fallen from her horse outside. She approves as Jonathan takes her clothes off and dresses her in jewels instead, but he cannot unfasten her chastity belt. Then he discovers a black tooth in her mouth, and a moment later in his frustration, he suspects "you have only come here to make me into a laughing-stock" (31). The woman is angry: "Three minutes ago you could have possessed my body: but instead you have tried to take possession of *me*; I am altogether to large for you" (32). She removes all his jewels except a belt, successfully unfastens the chastity belt, and jumps out of the window into a blanket held by the Dark Men. Jonathan, alone again, observes: "I am not yet defeated."

Critics, responding to the play's brevity and small cast, mostly judged it slight.[10] The piece is artificial, with its very literary language; and its world is unreal, unconvincing even as the distant past, unlike *Left-Handed Liberty*; and thinking of the Middle Ages and chivalric conventions of courtly love does not help to make the woman plausible. The title suggests a ballad, and the plot is that of "The Raggle-Taggle Gypsies": a dream-world where mysterious women from remote countries ride out of the mist. Jonathan represents a traditional order which will be overthrown—an order which has long outlived its usefulness, yet lingers on because of the strength of its walls and weapons. He chooses to be solitary and fearful, to think money buys everything, to wait for what he wants to turn up rather than to go out on a search, to prefer the dream of a woman to the reality, and to draw back when the prize is almost in his grasp. He thus contrasts in every way with the values of life, love, and spontaneity that are represented by the woman and the Dark Men. This is a familiar Arden contrast and one that is emphasized by size (the woman is mountainous; he is small) and color (he has red hair and yellow teeth; she is white and the men outside black). Even here anarchy's victory is partial, as Jonathan still holds the tower and its treasure.[11]

Chapter Seven
Trafalgar to Muswell Hill, 1968–70

The Hero Rises Up

After Arden accepted a commission early in 1965 to write the book of a musical about Lord Nelson, to be called *Trafalgar*, he and Margaretta D'Arcy undertook a substantial amount of research. He described this venture into a new form: "It's going to be a serious musical, by which I don't mean a solemn musical. It's really a character study of a particular kind of naval genius. Nelson is a very strange man when you juxtapose his successful naval career with his very odd and not very happy private life. And it is a play that seems to me to be raising a lot of issues that one might call serious."[1] The American composers of *Fiddler on the Roof*, Jerry Bock and Sheldon Harnick, wrote the music; and original plans were for a full-scale West End musical. Arden's ideas gradually altered, however, and he came to see the whole as "intimate," as ideally with semi-round staging like that in the off-Broadway cafe in which he had seen Barbara Garson's *Macbird*. He consequently could not agree with Bock and Harnick, and in February, 1968, the collaboration ended.

Arden and D'Arcy then rewrote their part as *The Hero Rises Up* and directed it themselves, with Institute of Contemporary Arts backing, in November, 1968, in the Round House, a Victorian locomotive-shed in North London. The play was seen again the following summer, presented by Nottingham Playhouse at Edinburgh Festival and in Nottingham, and it was given on radio in May, 1970.

"An Academic Representative of the Authors" begins *The Hero Rises Up* by asking, "Let us consider the last un-

100

contested hero-figure of our own history—Lord Nelson."[2] Whereupon Nelson bursts on stage through a screen, lists his victories, and sings of his conservative monarchist faith and the two themes, war and love: "I broke the rules of warfare / And the nation did forgive: / But there was no forgiveness when / I broke the rules of love" (17). The rest of the first, and best, act takes place in Naples in 1799. The king has been driven out by the French and a republican government led by Caracciolo established. Nelson recaptures Naples and has Caracciolo hanged, as the king demands. As the corpse is raised on the ship's yardarm, Nelson dances more and more sensuously with the loving Emma, Lady Hamilton, and Nelson's servant links the two events: "To get them to bed a man must hang!" (39). Nelson returns triumphant to England, greets his wife perfunctorily, and publicly associates with Emma. The centerpiece of the second act is a grand, drunken party at which Emma performs her famous series of "Attitudes," such as "the Spirit of Peace aware of the threat of Strife," and dances a tarantella, after which they all descend on the library and burn radical books. Nelson returns to sea and destroys the Danish navy at Copenhagen in 1801, then is seen back in England coping with an irritating group of his relatives. When he is killed winning at Trafalgar in 1805, his stepson points out how "barbaric" the battle-plan was. The final scene is Nelson's apotheosis; rising to the heavens in a gilded marine-chariot, he is accompanied by both Emma and Lady Nelson. The stepson says bitterly, like Walsh in *Musgrave*: "Equality, Fraternity and so on never came: / And where we were then, now we are just the same" (101). Nelson has the last word: "The hero rises up to reach / His everlasting proud reward" (101).

The "Asymmetrical Authors' Preface" develops an argument that the Celts were "curvilinear" people (approximately, emotional and romantic) and that the Romans introduced to Britain less desirable "rectilinear" qualities, of reason and classicism. This theory not only indicates the true character of Britons but also helps explain Nelson, the structure of the play (in the perspective of looking back from the present), and the way the Ardens want it staged ("we meant to write a play which need not be done properly," (5)).

For *The Hero Rises Up* the Ardens have attempted to find a new way of staging a history, one in which the play will involve its audience and be more than an entertainment. The form, ballad opera, uses numerous traditional tunes as *The Beggars' Opera* did, while the subtitle is "a Romantic Melodrama." The final ascension should suggest "popular two-pence coloured prints" of the toy theater, and Ronald Eyre observes: "Anyone who has sat as a child in front of a toy-theatre and willed a cut-out paper villain to do something villainous will have no difficulties with this style of playing."[3] The first production, which also included continuous film projections and electronic percussion, may have distracted from both the period manner and the content. The later Nottingham production found a different style, as Ronald Bryden explained, by sustituting "for the rough ballad-opera framework of the original, a period equivalent of the crude china mementoes of Nelson's death, a more sophisticated lampoon-style borrowing from music hall and Gilbert and Sullivan. But it makes the piece undeniably livelier, and allows to emerge from the Ardens' over-enthusiastic stylisation several scenes of subtle, distinguished poetic writing."[4]

Prose, verse, and song have distinct functions. Prose is used for most of the immediate action, such as the arguments at Naples and at the drunken party; and Nelson speaks prose in his official military duties. Verse reveals more sensitive aspects of character: Caracciolo has a long and lofty verse, the cultured Hamilton almost always speaks verse, appropriate for his spiritual nature, and Nelson turns to a gentle verse during his moments of regret and reflection. Songs provide a chorus for background information, satirical comment, and comic ditties about Nelson and Emma—short, pithy statements such as "She was barely more than twelve years old / When first upon her back she was rolled" (58).

While Arden had written before of historical figures such as Lindsay and King John, Nelson is closer in time and more fully documented. The Ardens' facts are highly selective but correct about Emma's colorful past (57–58, 89) and about Nelson's earlier career (41). Emma quotes a letter written by an uncle when Nelson first became a midshipman (40).

Nelson did in fact return his wife's last letter marked "opened by mistake by Lord Nelson, but not read" (92), and he did leave Emma as "a legacy to my King and Country" (97). As for Nelson's conduct in the first act, he could not only have saved Caracciolo's life but forced a moderate settlement on the King of Naples. There is no evidence, however, that the execution led to the seduction of Emma or that she urged him into bloodthirstiness. And Caracciolo's corpse did float to the surface during the king's return.[5] The Ardens present events in black and white, and they turn Naples under Caracciolo into a progressive society to be unhesitatingly approved.

The British know of Nelson as the man who had a sustained, public affair with a fat, vulgar, aging woman, and as the admiral who turned a blind eye to signals in a battle, who gave the message "England expects" at Trafalgar and was killed there, saying "Kiss me, Hardy," then was honored as a hero on a column in the center of London. This man is the Nelson of whom Robert Graves writes in "1805" ("By his unServicelike familiar ways, Sir, / He made the whole Fleet love him, damn his eyes!") and Lawrence Durrell in "A Ballad of the Good Lord Nelson": "Now stiff on a pillar with a phallic air / Nelson stylites in Trafalgar Square / Reminds the British what once they were / Aboard the Victory, Victory O."

In the Preface Nelson is placed as a man who "wasted his extraordinary energy, courage, and humanity upon having men killed" (5). Bryden identifies the two faces of Nelson depicted: "It is a serious portrait and a serious argument: the real Nelson, the true hero whom the British still adore, was not the stiff-backed slave of duty who executed Caracciolo, but the fallible, contradictory human being who flouted authority, bent regulations to suit himself and loved a fat, pretty demimondaine better than his wife. It is a simplified picture, but not without truth."[6] Albert Hunt expresses the debit side more harshly: "Nelson is a swashbuckling, carefree, romantic character who is also a criminal. Arden presents these contradictory facets to you and invites you to make your own judgment: if you prefer to ignore the criminality and succumb to the charm, that's your affair."[7] Since Nelson applies his Celtic "curvilinear" temperament not only to his private life but also to his Roman "rectilinear" job, he is a force for disorder within the system. He relishes life, like Sailor Sawney, Butterthwaite, and Armstrong; but he regrettably also relishes violence.

Nelson himself sings "I'm a hero" (45), his wife sings "He is the hero of this land" (78), Emma crowns him as "the Victor of the War" (59), and he is even hailed to the tune of "God save the Queen" (49). Arden challenges the reputation of "the last uncontested hero figure" by showing his conduct at Naples as deplorable; that, if he was a hero at Copenhagen, it was through disobeying orders; and that, if a hero at Trafalgar, through savage inhumanity. His personal life, defying convention, might show a kind of heroism, but such courage must be balanced by his cruelty to Lady Nelson. His short stature is cut down further when a servant controls what he can drink and when old Hamilton ejects his unruly relatives. The author's own ambivalence may be seen: as a sympathizer with pacifism and anarchism, he does not want heroes; when identifying with the revolutionary Left, he responds to the potency of Che Guevara and Mao Tse-tung, who are named in the Prologue.

Arden comments that "The British public prefers to do without wars and to make love whenever it can. The top brass cannot do without wars and has nothing to do with love. Nelson belonged to both categories."[8] So to the 1960s cry of "Make Love, not War," Arden offers the man who made love and war, one who may even have had to make war if he was to be able to make love—which could also be a comment on the unknown motives of some other warmakers of past and present. Here Arden also draws a distinction between the ruling class and the masses when he mentions the hypocritical way in which the "rectilinear" "top brass" actually treated its hero's last wish: generous grants went to his wife, brother, and sisters; but Emma received nothing. The "curvilinear" British public are seen as the press-ganged ships' crews and as Allen, who is forgotten at the end, then promoted to bosun and expected to be grateful.

In *The Hero Rises Up* the Ardens bring together three elements of the Nelson story: the endearing humanity of the lovers, the issues of the Napoleonic Wars, and Nelson's conduct at Naples, which British admirers usually conveniently forget. Nevertheless, the intellectual content is less varied and searching than in the earlier historical plays. As theatrical experiment, this play tries to find a style of the period described, to make form reinforce content. Yet this form of fairground booths, puppets, and toy-theater cutouts imposes simple, bold, and crude effects, so the Ardens could not go very deeply into characterizing Nelson and his times or present meditations about true heroism.

The Bagman

Arden's work in the years after completing *Left-Handed Liberty* shows two tendencies. He began to control productions himself, a happy experience with *The Royal Pardon* but a more chequered one with *The Hero Rises Up*. Other works—the "War Carnival" at New York University and "Harold Muggins Is a Martyr"—show directly a clear-cut political and social standpoint. Yet he still believed that he was avoiding total commitments and was tempted to indulge his poetic and artistic instincts. *The Bagman* expresses his crises of conscience of these years.

The Bagman, written in the spring of 1969, is Arden's return to radio for the first time since "The Life of Man" thirteen years ealier. When the Narrator leaves his home in Muswell Hill to buy a newspaper, he announces that he is: "John Arden (thirty-eight) of ancient family, / Writer of plays for all the world to see, / To see, and pay for, and to denigrate: / Such was my work since 1958."[9] He falls asleep in a nearby park where an old gypsy woman sells him a kit bag and hints that it may contain a willing girl. When the park-keeper turns him out, his surroundings change to a lonely moor, where a group of starving women surround a corpse. They attack him, and he is rescued by some mounted soldiers, who take him to a "slovenly and uncared-for" town (48). He watches an entertainment and a scramble for candies, dried beans, and pearls, and he is then dragged on stage himself. He opens his bag and tips out "little men and little women, the largest of them about twelve inches long, made out of wood and carefully jointed and carved. Each one of them dressed in a characteristic costume" (57). When the manikins act out a violent drama of a mass revolt against the ruling class, they are defeated and later successful, but their success is followed by a quarrel among the victors. The Narrator sleeps until awakened by a Young Woman, who describes the nature of the society—the prosperous in the city, the poor outside, and the country dependent on the goodwill of a king overseas. After an unsuccessful escape attempt, the Narrator is taken to see the king's Ambassador, and then to the king, who demands entertainment, whereupon the little figures present an indecent, erotic show.

After some time, the Narrator wakes from a dream within the dream and the Young Woman shows him the true king, an old man chained to a wall. They go underground and join a resistance group: "for the first time for how many hundreds of years it is power we are going to get," she says (83). Told to take up a weapon, the Narrator says of his bag of little men, "This *is* my weapon!" (85); but the figures are unhappy and will not perform. The guerillas, distracted by his art, are attacked and he wakes, with an empty kit bag. Walking home, he reflects: "It would have been easy it would have been good / To have carried a bag full of solid food / And fed the thin men till they were / As fat as the men who held them in fear." And he ends: "All I can do is to look at what I see" (88).

When *The Bagman* was broadcast on March 27, 1970, directed by Martin Esslin, the listeners were enthusiastic: David Wade found "the quality of a large, vital and slightly sinister poster," and Peter Porter called it "a true work of art and a rare piece of radio."[10]

Arden's commission when he wrote *The Bagman* was to write a companionpiece for a broadcast of Eugene Ionesco's *L'Impromptu d'Alma* (better known by its subtitle, *The Shepherd's Chameleon*). Ionesco's play echoes the titles of Molière's *L'Impromptu de Versailles* (1663) and Jean Giraudoux's *L'Impromptu de Paris* (1937), both dramatizations of their own theories of art that ridicule others' theories. Arden shows the link with his subtitle, *The Impromptu of Muswell Hill*, and offers an analogy as his view of creativity. To him, his artistic ability is an undreamed-of and unlooked-for gift. The figures given to him are made to act by his speaking "in a strange distorted voice" (58), but what they do is outside his control. Their performance is suited to their audience: violence for the town masses, eroticism for the ruling class, and nothing to give the rebels who direct him to abandon his bag. *The Bagman*, while a haunting and intriguing tale, is also a nightmare: listeners are shocked by this dream-world which has too many parallels with present-day reality.

Because the world is one of cruelty, suffering, and oppression, the artist cannot be contented with presiding over his figures. Hence *The Bagman* is urgent, anguished, and highly personal. The conclusion is an apparent acceptance of the Narrator's nature, which is suited only for observing and not for full involvement. But earlier the Ambassador has said that the Narrator is perhaps "a hedger and a fencesitter, and a contemptible poltroon" (74). In Arden's Introduction, written two years later, he explains how this assessment was true for him: "A prestige position on a pacifist newspaper was, I came to feel, at any rate for myself, a classic piece of Fence-Sitting" (13–14). Hence, with the changed insights brought about by the visit to India, "The attitude of the central character at the end of the story is reprehensible, cowardly, and not to be imitated" (17). Arden's new position of unqualified support for the thin men against the fat is expressed for the first time in his next play *The Ballygombeen Bequest*.

Chapter Eight
Camelot, 1972
"Keep Those People Moving!"

"Keep Those People Moving!," commissioned by British Broadcasting Corporation schools' radio for a series for five-year-olds, *Let's Join In*, was heard in two twenty-minute parts on November 24 and December 1, 1972. "Keep Those People Moving!" tells a version of the Nativity story in the simplest language, beginning: "Today I'm going to tell you the story about Joseph and Mary. Joseph made tables and chairs and doors and window-frames for people's houses. He wasn't a rich man. One day Mary told him that she was going to have a baby—and that she thought the baby would be born at the end of the year—in the middle of the cold weather." After a policeman has told Joseph that he has to pay tax and must go to Bethlehem to pay it, Joseph goes to a café to discuss his problem with friends. A Stranger comes to Mary and asks: "Then give your son to us—to the friends of the poor people—in time to come they will need / A strong young man to lend them strength when they themselves are tired and weary, / And can no longer stand up against these bad kings and their cruelty." The title song follows:

Keep those people moving on, keep those people on the go
The more they walk, the less they can talk, the less they know.
If they know nothing, there is nothing they can do.
The king is the king and he will rule
If the people ever stop to ask the reason why
The king will fall and the king will die.

The poor start to plan to kill the rich, oppressive King Herod, who is frightened until he has the idea of exhausting and dispersing the people by requiring them to return to

108

their birthplaces to pay their taxes. Joseph and Mary are heard seeking a room in Bethlehem and finally finding the stable. Jesus is born, and Mary sings to him: "Joshua fought the people's fight, but the people fought it too / Jesus, if you have to stand up and fight, will the people fight with you?" The shepherds and "three well-dressed serious-looking old gentlemen" visit the baby. When Herod discovers that "the eldest children of all the families are being taught to hate their king, to hate him and to kill him—once they have all grown up, that is what they are going to do," he orders the killing of all young children. Finally, the Stranger returns to warn Mary, and her family flee to safety in Egypt.

Although the Ardens relate some of the Bible story simply and attractively enough, they add their slant by showing opposition to Herod's tyranny and by making angels into couriers for guerilla groups. They have created, in fact, a secular nativity play about the birth of a revolutionary, and Anthony Thwaite has rightly observed the oddity of presenting the Christmas story as "entirely concerned with the struggles of the over-taxed and oppressed poor against a nasty despot."[1]

The Island of the Mighty

Arden first worked on a play about King Arthur as early as 1953; a version rewritten in 1955–56 was rejected by the Royal Court Theater. Ten years later he was commissioned to writed a trilogy for television and wrote on the same subject; however, by the time the work was completed, British Broadcasting Corporation policies had changed and it was refused. He rewrote the work for the stage while in India in 1970, particularly emphasizing religious beliefs. The following year, as he explains in his Preface, it was written yet again, this time in collaboration with D'Arcy and reflecting new interests in the economic structure of a tribal society. For performance, more than a third of the text had to be cut; part 3 was reduced to a short epilogue; but the running time was almost four hours. The play, directed by David Jones and presented by the Royal Shakespeare Company at the Aldwych in London, opened on December 5, 1972.

The production was stormy. Arden was paid to attend rehearsals so that he could help with cuts and revisions. After six weeks of rehearsal and two weeks before the first night, D'Arcy arrived, saw a run-through, and protested that an anti-imperialist piece was being staged as pro-imperialist. The Ardens demanded a meeting with the cast to discuss the issue, and, when the cast voted against holding a meeting, the Ardens walked out. They announced that, as members of the Society of Irish Playwrights, they were on strike; they picketed the theater; and they unsuccessfully attempted to make a protest on stage during a preview. Thus later cuts in the text performed were not approved by the Ardens.[2]

The Island of the Mighty is set "early in the Sixth Century," a hundred years after the Romans left Britain. The island is divided among several semi-independent princes, who are in varying degrees Christian and Romanized. Arthur, the Red Dragon General and the victor in twelve great battles, is now a seventy-year-old hobbling on a stick. His Chief Poet, Merlin, explains: "In his lineage and language he is both Roman and Briton. By religion he is Christian, and his work is to defend civility and Christianity from one end of the Island to the other."[3]

In part 1, "Two Wild Young Noblemen," Arthur is faced with three problems. The English (more commonly known as Angles or Anglo-Saxons) from Germany are likely to invade in the northeast. Second, a descendant of Romans, Pellam, has pronounced himself King in the Wirral, in the central northwest. Third, the pagan Wild Cat Picts in Galloway in Scotland are in conflict with the ruler of the area, Strathclyde, Arthur's nephew. Arthur turns first on Pellam and defeats him. The Picts, however, win the first skirmish with Strathclyde because Arthur sends little help.

The story of the wild young noblemen, Balin and Balan, interweaves with this planning and fighting. These twins set out together to join Arthur, but they quarrel and only Balin does so. Next day Balin impulsively kills the princess who is the Picts' ambassador, making war with them unavoidable. He travels on to see Pellam, and wounds him with his sacred spear, then journeys on again by boat. His brother Balan, meanwhile, has joined the Picts, becoming one of them by accepting a large cat-mask. Forced to fight and kill their Sacred King, Balan rules for a year and a day until it is his turn to be killed. Balin is shipwrecked nearby and forced to fight the new Sacred King. They kill each other and, before dying, they discover that they are brothers.

Part 2, "Oh the Cruel Winter," the most complicated section, begins with a meeting of the Chief Poets. The poem presented by Aneurin, Chief Poet to Gododdin, ruler of southwest Scotland, outrages them. Meanwhile, Arthur and another of his nephews, Medraut, discover that the invading English claim to have Gododdin's permission to settle in this region, so Arthur visits Gododdin to discuss the problem. On arrival he impulsively marries Gwenhwyvar, Gododdin's sister. Medraut stays behind and recruits a force of skirmishers.

Then old Morgan, Arthur's half-sister, enters and explains how two thousand years earlier the Blessed Hero Bran had slept with his sister Branwen and the line had continued ever since through women. Now, she says, "the dragonbanner must be broken and the Daughters of Branwen called home" (149). Morgan proclaims Gwenhwyvar the Daughter of Branwen. Whoever Gwenhwyvar chooses will be "the Secret King of the Island of the Mighty, he will be Bran, reincarnate" (150); she chooses Medraut. Aneurin, who is thrilled that the Daughter of Branwen is revealed, predicts that she can rule through love alone in a new Golden Age. Medraut and Gwenywyvar together proclaim the restored Kingdom of Branwen and lead this new force, pre-Roman and pre-Christian in spirit, against Arthur. The battle of Camlann follows, and Aneurin describes how the English invaders defeated both Medraut, who is killed, and Arthur's army. The dying Arthur staggers across the stage with a broken sword and Merlin, now insane, has the last word: "Merlin is a bird!" (171).

"A Handful of Watercress," part 3, is, in Aneurin's words, "The tale of one who lived / And ran stark crazy in his pain" (175), Merlin. A flashback to the night before the battle shows Merlin killing Taliesin, formerly Strathclyde's Chief Poet; before he dies, Taliesin curses Merlin to wander like a wild bird. Bedwyr, with Arthur's broken sword, is next seen leading the small defeated army back to Carlisle, where he orders Aneurin to find Merlin and imprisons the woman who was once Merlin's wife, Gwenddydd. When Aneurin meets old Morgan, she takes him to the Glen of the Madmen where they find Merlin, and she briefly restores his sanity by tickling and crooning to him. Then Merlin and Morgan run through the countryside until she falls off a cliff. Bedwyr continues retreating into Picts' country, accompanied by Aneurin, who is now living with Gwenddydd. Merlin, living outdoors, is fed by a friendly Cowman's wife; but, when the jealous Cowman finds them together, he kills Merlin. Finally, Aneurin quotes the resurrected Lazarus speaking of the corpses he had known: "We are going to come back / And we are going to take hold / So hideous and bloody greedy / We take hold of the whole world!"

The Ardens in their notes recommend performing the play on "a light platform . . . in the middle of the acting area" so that "actors seen approaching it, or waiting beside it for their cues, can be in or out of character according to circumstances, thereby breaking down any intense subjective/naturalistic/historical/poetical/classical sentiments which may have been begotten in them" (23). Eight different backcloths, such as Fort, Camp, and Raid, serve as "emblems of the kind of environment" for each scene, and the Ardens provide rough sketches to guide the design. The earlier Notes, which differ a little on the number and design of backcloths, suggest not only nets, floor cloths, Celtic designs on the stage wings, but also a number of "Signs," such as Wild Cat, Mermaid, and Millwheel, to establish context. The Ardens ask for two or three musicians on the forestage to play percussion throughout. They stress that the style must be "as direct as the period" (25), "as athletic and rapid and light" as possible (23). The full text, which has thirty-three characters, also needs Companions, other Chief Poets, some Monks, Messengers, fighters, peasants, madmen and women, and soldiers' wives.

The Ardens' Preface names as sources Geoffrey of Monmouth, Thomas Malory (particularly for Balin and Balan of part 1), and the Irish epic *Crazy Sweeney*. David Jones, director of the Aldwych production, cites *Roman Britain and the*

English Settlements by R. G. Collingwood and J. N. L. Myres (1936), as providing Arden's view of the status of Arthur: a Romanized, roving cavalry commander serving the various British princes against invasions. Arden defies tradition in locating Arthur in Carlisle rather than in southwest England, but he has some scholarly support for this change. Jones additionally mentions J. G. Frazer's *Golden Bough* and Jessie Weston's *From Ritual to Romance* for the Maimed King rite and the *Mabinogion*[4] for the line "Because the knife has gone into the meat and the drink into the horn and there is a congregation of guests in Arthur's hall tonight" (43). The *Mabinogion* provides the story of Branwen, important in part 2, and refers frequently to Britain as "the Island of the Mighty." The Ardens are also familiar with Aneurin's epic-elegy *Gododdin*, for example. The names indicate their preference for the early Welsh sources rather than Malory: Gwenhwyvar is better known as Guinevere, Medraut as Mordred, and Bedwyr as Bedevere.

Three leads on the meanings of the drama are offered by the Ardens. The program note states the first:

"The Matter of Britain is the story of what happened after the Roman Imperial administration had been withdrawn from this island. The Britons reverted to a tribalism, which, although politically inept and self-destructive, was accompanied by a strong sense of liberty and individual pride.[5]

This statement about the social and economic history of post-Roman Britain comments on a world known more from myth and legend than from historical fact. Arden makes clear that Arthur was wrong in maintaining Roman imperialism even after the Empire had collapsed. Thus the tribalism which has taken its place is admirable because it expresses liberty and pride, and even Gododdin's tolerance of the arrival of the English is good because benefits will eventually follow. Presumably, though, a return to the age-old uniting spirit of Bran and Branwen would be even better, yet, disastrously, Medraut does not genuinely adopt this spirit.

Arthur, then, is debunked: he is not a tragic and romantic hero any more than Nelson was in Arden's previous historical play. Arthur places himself as "a careful and Christian General, who alone among his countrymen has read books full of good sense. Titus Livius, Julius Caesar" (108). Like Musgrave, Arthur knows his only duty is fighting: "I am a soldier, I make war, with good conscience, and that's it" (128). Like Lindsay, he knows he can achieve no more than short-term peace, for the pressure on European tribes by others moving westward is continuous. In the past, at the time of his incestuous relation with a Daughter of Branwen, he was wilder; but he is now rational and reasonable—but also tired and old. In the second part he has to prove himself in love with Gwenhwyvar before planning a new war; but his love fails when she taunts his religion. Arthur is a rectilinear man faced with curvilinear people, Celts. Arden believes, as David Jones remarks, that "a society which consists entirely of discipline and repression is an unhealthy society."[6]

The program note, on the second meaning of the drama, directs the audience to the common people and to their relevance to the Third World in the twentieth century:

National myths of this sort present a picture of a way of life remarkably similar to that which exists today in the "Third World". . . . Just as the energy of Britain in the sixth century was concentrated among the wild tribesmen of the hills and the crude English just stepped from their black ships, so the Third World contains—to our alarm and perhaps our ultimate salvation—the strongest urge for social change and the keenest courage in bringing it about.[7]

In the Notes on Costume the Ardens stress that the downtrodden poor should be distinct: "There would be a very clear and observable difference between the dresses of the rich and poor. . . . The essential precept to bear in mind in dressing these plays is Lenin's famous question: 'Who? Whom?' Who, for example, derives his income at the expense of whom, and how is this demonstrated in their personal appearance?" (24, 25).

The suffering poor frequently appear: Caradoc, a smallholder whose cows were killed by soldiers (135–36); a Farmer stuggling on, using corpses for fertilizer, after his house, wife, and beasts have been burned (193–94); and the refugees. The Ardens' panorama includes a Miller who knows the importance of his work: "My trade is to grind up corn, I have my wheels here with their great teeth: they are the good tools of my trade. When you are dead and all your sons are dead, this craftwork will be needed, by the heathen English or whoever else" (200). The bandit and the Bond-woman of the first part represent the harsh fight for existence of those outside any settled society. The Picts have energy, but "the true voice of liberty" is not clearly heard from Arden's huddled masses.

A third theme mentioned in the Notes is "the relationship of the poet to society. In the old Celtic civilization the poets played an important role in shaping the politics of the community."[8] *The Bagman* revealed Arden's own urgent concern with this issue. *The Island of the Mighty*, apart from the comic members of the College of Bards in the second part, has four Chief Poets who can be compared. The Pictish poet is, in David Jones's words, "a bard whose function in his community is still basically religious, he's the keeper of the rites, the observer of the rituals, a kind of High Priest."[9] Aneurin has work, as banker and letter-writer (105), which is separate from his own untraditional poems: he is delighted to have his songs spread orally and is unconcerned about fame (106). Taliesin has lost his poetic instincts and strives to be a peacemaker: "The highest function of our traditional craft is the mediation of peace. We must walk between the armies and persuade them by our rhetoric" (169).

Merlin, narrator and probably the play's most important character, has a firm sense of his duty to promote Arthur's greatness: "So many have heard the songs / I have made about Arthur my general / So many more will remember them and / Remember my name when I am dead" (106). When Merlin stands beside the dead Bondwoman, he ago-nizes about poetry and war: "I am the General's Poet—I make / The words that make him famous in his age— / . . . My words are ever willing / In the service of his sword" (86). Merlin pathetically hopes he can begin to be a full and proper poet when Morgan restores his sanity, and Aneurin says Merlin should have been a private poet instead of a public bard: "He desired to be a poet: he desired to make a song. / He desired to make it for himself alone / And for a girl, could he find one to love" (213). Merlin dies mad; and John Peter observes, "The pitiful animal degradation of the artist who had once sold his soul is one of the starkest and most original passages in modern drama."[10]

A few critics were driven to hysterical anger, among them Harold Hobson, who exploded about "boring, pedantic, self-indulgent, show-off balderdash."[11] Other critics were hostile because they sought in vain for intellectual coherence, like J. W. Lambert: "I should be happy if I could extract, as I certainly could not, some general drift from the piece."[12] Some reviewers, trying less hard to extract a drift, enjoyed it; they responded to the telling of strange stories in an exotic setting: " 'Tales told by Merlin and other poets' might have been a more accurate title," observed Frank Marcus, while B. A. Young found it "immensely exciting and deeply poetic."[13]

The Island of the Mighty carefully juxtaposes song and poetry, the prose of planning and information, and big visual effects such as the rituals of the Picts, the mating of Arthur and Gwenhwyvar, and the proclamation of the Kingdom of Bran. But the episodes appear merely juxtaposed, the focus shifts, and characters come and go: most of the main figures at the start—Balin, Balan, Pellam, the bandit, the Bond-woman—are dead by the end of part 1. This is a rich canvas, like Malory's, but the book can be put down when the reader has had enough. Unfamiliar myth and strange gnomic poetic utterances occur too often. Part 3—a bleak vision of a disordered wintry world of poets and madmen, a prophetic old woman, and uncertain defeated knights—is self-contained enough to be worth staging on its own. One layer of interest is simply laid on top of others: early in 1969 the themes were stated as the poet in society and as the decline of imperialism.[14] Myth and religion add another layer, and the visit to India adds the forms of tribalism, the problems of the Third World, and a Marxist view of history. The Ardens' ambition—presenting a whole civilization and refashioning the first and greatest myth of Britain—is colossal; but the execution is confusing.

Chapter Nine
The Ardens' Ireland, and Radio Plays, 1972–82

The Little Gray Home in the West

The Ardens' move to County Galway in 1971 soon led to a public response to Irish issues. Arden responded vigorously to the conflict in Northern Ireland, which erupted violently in August, 1969, and has continued ever since, commenting, for example, that in Britain there was little reporting of the oppression of Catholics or of Army misconduct.[1] The perspective, as so often, was historical and now shaped by Marxism: "As regards Ireland I want to see a non-sectarian socialist republic eventually established which will—for the first time in recorded history— give the workers full control over the enjoyment of the fruits of their labour."[2]

In Fall, 1971, the Ardens heard about the case of Mrs. Fahey in the small town of Oughterard, close to where they lived. She was an old widow facing eviction by an absentee landlord from the cottage in which her family had lived for 150 years. "A legal quibble," wrote Arden, "was evoked which effectively did her out of her title to the cottage and the adjacent field." Mrs. Fahey appealed, maintaining that the agreement was invalid becau_e her husband was ill and under the influence of drink when he signed. Local protest at the eviction was resisted by the hoteliers, men were beaten up, a meeting was disrupted, and workers were blacklisted.[3] The Ardens saw this as just one small part of the struggle between the thin men and the fat, already conspicuous in Oughterard when land had been used for a golf course instead of farming.

117

Margaretta D'Arcy borrowed the legal documents on the Fahey case, and the Ardens decided to write a play together based on the episode, quickly, as "a weapon in the agitation." *The Ballygombeen Bequest*, subtitled "an Anglo-Irish melodrama," resulted. Charles Marowitz's Open Space Theater in London has asked Arden for a play about the Ulster conflict, but *The Bequest* was acrimoniously rejected. The play instead was first read early in 1972 at the all-Ireland university drama festival in Galway, at which Arden served, controversially, as adjudicator. The first performance followed on May 1 by students of St. Joseph's & St. Mary's Colleges of Education Dramatic Societies in Falls Road, Belfast. *The Bequest* was subsequently staged by the 7:84 Company, at Edinburgh Festival and on a tour which included two short visits to London, to the small Bush Theater. The program included a seven-page manifesto with the name, address, and phone number of the alleged culprit. The Ardens were sued for libel, and most papers avoided possible law-breaking by not reviewing the play. The court case was finally heard in the fall of 1977, with the Ardens eventually apologizing and settling out of court.[4] They rewrote the play as *The Little Gray Home in the West*. This was read at the Sugawn Theater, Highbury, London, on May 4, 1978, then first performed by the Birmingham University Drama Department in January, 1982.[5]

The text summarized and discussed here is *The Little Gray Home in the West*, since this is available as a book. *The Ballygombeen Bequest*, though printed only in the American periodical *Scripts*, may, however, represent what the Ardens really wished to write. In both versions the main subject is absentee landlord versus poor Irish tenant, to which the Ardens add the torture and death of an I.R.A. suspect in Northern Ireland and some broader context of Irish history and current Irish politics.

The play shows a villain with a bit of the swagger of Krank of *Waters of Babylon* in Baker-Fortescue, an English businessman. He declares, in one of the passages in irregular rhyming verse:

> I am not rich, but I have always found
> That where a lawyer creeps upon the ground

Profits accrue, emoluments abound.
Whatever news he sends me by this post
I have no fear but I shall soon acquire
Some crafty carving-knife with which to rule the roast!
I am, you see, a business-man;
I look to the main chance where I can.[6]

After the war he inherits a chalet and fifteen acres in Kilnas-leeveen, which he rents to wealthy visitors. Sick, drunken Seamus, ever-pregnant Teresa, and their children have for generations occupied rent-free a tumbledown cottage on the land in return for janitorial duties at the chalet. After some years, this becomes an agreement, signed by Seamus: he occupies the cottage for his lifetime. When he dies in 1968, Baker-Fortescue prepares to evict.

Teresa's son, Padraic, returns, just too late for his father's funeral, from a strike in Manchester, having learned there the concept of "Mass Support and the Solidarity of the Working Class" (46). "We are the people and the land belongs to us!" he adds (47), then quotes Lenin, "Educate, Agitate, Organise" (56). The plot grows complex in the second half, when secret agents from Dublin and from the British Ministry of Defence arrive. When Padraic goes into Northern Ireland to sell ponies, he is suspected of I.R.A. membership. British troops beat him up and he dies. His sister sings over the corpse:

> They butchered him like Connolly
> Or Emmet or Wolfe Tone
> Or a thousand thousand other ones
> Who likewise are all gone!
> The martyrs that you shout about
> Roll over in their graves
> But those alive you do not know
> Bewildered work like slaves—
> They cannot tell for whom they work
> Or why they draw their pay:
> All that they have is martyred bones
> And glorious names to praise. (70–71)

The story ends briskly. Old Teresa will lose her court case because of a politically partisan judge, and she is given the

fare to join her sister in England. The chalet is blown up and
the local contractor buys the site. The dead Padraic incites a
fight with custard pies on a stage full of flying bank notes
between the contractor and Baker-Fortescue, then he dances
and sings with his sister and mother:

> When you act in a play it is easy to say
> That we shall win and never be defeated
> When you go from here it is not so clear
> That power for the people is predestined.
> Giddy-i-ay but don't forget
> Giddy-i-ay you must remember
> Giddy-i-ay tiddle-iddle-oo
> There are more of us than them! (73)

Though the scenes and story of *The Little Gray Home in
the West* are much the same as that of *The Ballygombeen Bequest*, the bulk of the text has been revised, with various
cuts, additions, and changed emphases. To eliminate the
libel, the name, occupation, and hometown of the English
landowner have been changed, and the eviction occurs in
Munster instead of in Connacht. Padraic and the Narrator
become a single character, with Padraic opening and thus
framing the play. Only *The Ballygombeen Bequest* directs:
"The entire play should be accompanied by music . . . in
order to accentuate the rhythm of the spoken dialogue and
the action."[7] The scenes in the later text acquire Brechtian
titles, and more Irish history is introduced, notably a parallel
between Baker-Fortescue tricking Seamus into signing away
his land and Lloyd George in 1921 securing Michael Collins's
signature to the treaty creating the Irish Free State.

Critics who saw *The Ballygombeen Bequest* in 1972 divided on the emphasis they gave to the message of the play,
and on whether or not they found this message sympathetic.
Robert Brustein hated it: "Its ends are . . . quite chillingly inhuman. . . . With such a work, [Arden] is no longer con-
tributing to art but rather to what George Orwell called 'the
smelly little orthodoxies that are nowadays contending for
our souls.' "[8] Charles Lewsen defined it objectively as "a
timely political statement of total intellectual honesty."[9]
Michael Anderson enthusiastically welcomed play and

message as "a stunning political drama as good as the best of Arden and (let me stick my neck out) an equal to most of Brecht. . . . *The Ballygombeen Bequest* is more than a play about Ireland; it conjures up a nightmare image of capitalism, friendless, tottering and ultimately without hope or help."[10] Other reviewers were caught up in the excitement of the event: Jonathan Hammond found it "a tremendous theatrical experience" while John Lahr found the drama "takes the stage with incredible energy. . . . The stage is never just a platform for statement, but a fairground of activity. . . . [The actors] love this play for its craft as well as the humanity behind its political cunning."[11]

Some flourishes in the verse are typically Arden, e.g., "We met by chance on a lonely road / In a gap of the broken weather" (55); "Who is that man? I see him run—/ An ancient ragged bleeding man / Across the green mountain fast as he can" (26). The central conflict is also familiar, between soft, easy-living, educated townsfolk and nobler, rougher country people—Jackson-Sawney, Lindsay-Armstrong, and Jonathan-Dark Men again.

The scholarly interest in earlier dramatic forms and the desire to attempt something he has not attempted before show in the achievement here of a cheer-the-hero hiss-the-villain melodrama, in contrast to the idiosyncratic embroidery of melodrama in *The Workhouse Donkey*. Resisting the usual impulse toward subtlety, the Ardens have written here the work of wide appeal they tried for in *The Hero Rises Up*. Brustein comments that the night he saw the play "before a predominantly Irish audience in Shepherd's Bush, it was received with the fervour of an Agincourt harangue."[12] The song, dance, farce, and high spirits provide gaiety in the manner of Brendan Behan's *The Hostage* and some of Joan Littlewood's successes.

The Little Gray Home, further, is polemical as only "Harold Muggins" of earlier work was. The title suggests Abbey Theater peasant comedy, but paradoxically the Ardens are showing that the west of Ireland has real people and real problems, not just shebeens, priests, and beautiful green hills. What Seamus and Teresa need is a good modern house, large enough for their family, and picturesque thatch and sports fishing are irrelevant. The middle class—represented by the contractor who is also the government party's man in the district—have failed the Irish masses, while the government is preoccupied with questions of trade with Europe. The Englishman Baker-Fortescue is ultimately exploited by the Irish as were other English innocents in Ireland in Sean O'Casey's *Purple Dust*, with the political moral being drawn more clearly by Arden of the English middle class than by O'Casey of the Irish working class. Arden wants to be rid of age-old Irish mistrust of the English, for Padraic has to go to England to learn that the workers of the world must unite. In such savage verse as the following, the Ardens widen our horizon from their starting point of the eviction of an old Irish widow in Oughterard to rich versus poor worldwide:

> From the year of nineteen fifty-nine
> To nineteen sixty-eight
> The fat men of the fat half-world
> Had food on every plate.
> The lean men of the naked world
> Grew leaner every day
> And if they put their faces up
> Their teeth were kicked away. (41)

The Non-Stop Connolly Show

The Ardens' second Irish subject, James Connolly, occupied them for several years. Their forty-five-page essay in *To Present the Pretence* supplies a full account of the genesis and intentions of their play. They decided in 1969 that "the history of the one representative of Revolutionary International Socialism among the leaders of 1916 [the unsuccessful Easter Week Rising in Dublin] was undoubtedly the most important possible theme for an Irish play of the present day."[13] During 1971, when Arden was asked to write a radio play about a subject of his own choice, he selected Connolly. When, according to Arden, Esslin replied that such a play was undesirable because it might "inflame passions," Arden responded: "The reputation earned by Connolly in 1911 as a trade union organizer among the Protestant dockers of Belfast has not yet been entirely dimmed. The historical example of such a man today should serve to reduce pseudo-religious passions rather than inflame them."

Although Arden wrote explosively about this British Broadcasting Corporation "censorship,"[14] the Ardens' thinking turned to a stage play and eventually to a cycle of plays. The plays' evolution was shaped both by current local Irish issues and by the Ardens' experiences at Davis, California, in 1973, when they intended to write and stage the play about Connolly in the United States. The style was influenced by Brecht and by Hindu dramas they had seen in India.[15] Most of the *Non-Stop Connolly Show* is in prose, but the work is interspersed with songs and with rhyming and blank verse.

When the *Show* was finally completed late in 1974 as six plays, the first two had one long act each; the other four each had three acts. The program note for the London production summarized the Ardens' intentions to "clarify and explain many aspects of the Irish problem which at present mystify British audiences." As a result, the *Show* was long because of "the need to disentangle the many complex threads of social and political history involved in the Connolly story."[16] The Ardens' essay adds other insights: Connolly, for instance, was to be a hero without any tragic flaw. The struggles of Connolly's career would be presented fully and seriously: if "his years in the U.S.A. were dogged by a perpetual inability to see eye-to-eye on politics with the American Socialist De Leon, then we would dramatise this feud . . . as though it were, say, the quarrel between the rulers of the world in *Antony and Cleopatra*."[17] Finally, there was the Ardens' deep sense of the history, culture, and myths of Ireland: "We stated in a programme note that the dramaturgy of the show was influenced by traditional Irish forms. One well-known element in Celtic art is the intertwining of serpentine motifs. It is sometimes something of a puzzle to pick these out and follow them through."[18] Since the Ardens are deeply involved with both Socialism and current Irish issues, the appeal of Connolly to them is easily seen. The most significant part of his example may be his reconciliation of Socialism with both Roman Catholicism and Irish nationalism.

Part 1 of the *Show* presents Connolly's childhood in

Scotland, during which he obtains and loses three different
jobs, twice meets his uncle, an Irish rebel in hiding, and joins
the army and is sent to Ireland. After listening to a Socialist
agitator in Dublin he declares, "I am a man is now aware of
how this world is made!"[19] The opposition is represented by
Grabitall and three Employers, who appear in all six plays.
Connolly falls in love with Lillie and deserts the army to be
with her.

They return to Scotland together in part 2, and she sings
"In eighteen hundred and eighty-nine / It seemed as though
the glorious time / Of revolution was at the prime / In
England and in Scotland" (31). Connolly meets his brother
and John Leslie, two active Socialists, and becomes Secretary
of the Scottish Socialist Federation. Busying himself with
papers, he says, "If I am an oak tree my fingers are blunt
twigs on the ends of knotted branches / For the first time in
my lifetime a regular pen they must wield" (45). He works
hard, surprising himself with the success of his first speech,
then loses an election and his job. With two young children
to support, he is relieved when he is offered the job of
organizer for the Dublin Socialist Club.

In part 3 Connolly arrives in Dublin to find the club has
eight members and no money to pay him; however, he is
able to organize them as the Irish Socialist Republican Party
but once again has to look for work: "The Employers enter,
each with a placard reading 'Situations Vacant'. During the
song, Connolly approaches them one by one to ask for work,
but each time the placard is turned round and he reads the
inscription on the reverse: 'No Vacancies'. This becomes a
kind of *danse macabre*, the Employers enticing him on
deliberately to enjoy his disappointment" (10). Connolly
brings out *The Workers' Republic*, "the first socialist
newspaper to be published in Ireland" (31). When the Boer
War begins ("the fighting should be suggested symbolically
by the hurling of rolls of toilet paper and the like" [39]),
Connolly organizes protests. He goes to America to lecture
and a chorus-line enters, "(men in bow-ties and flat straw
hats, with canes: girls in fishnet tights with bunches of
feathers on their buttocks: one man representing a Railway-
Conductor with a peaked cap, a whistle to blow, and a flag).

They dance a routine in the manner of a travelling train, stopping between the stanzas of the song. Connolly, with a battered suitcase and his lecture notes, trots along the dancers, miming speeches at each pause" (69). After his return to Dublin, he quarrels with the Party, resigns, and decides to go back to the United States to work for Daniel De Leon's Socialist Labor Party.

When the cold, dictatorial De Leon proves unwelcoming, Connolly is forced to find work selling insurance at the start of part 4, which weaves together Connolly's experiences with the personalities on the Left in America between 1903 and 1910. The personalities include Big Bill Haywood, Mother Jones, Elizabeth Gurley Flynn, Samuel Gompers, and Eugene Debs. Among the subjects are whether Socialist sections formed by nationality are appropriate (Connolly forms an Irish one), the brief unity of the Left when Haywood is unjustly charged with murder, the rivalry between the American Federation of Labor and the International Workers of the World, and the 1908 election: "Eugene Debs, he's mounted to the cabin / Eugene Debs with his orders in his hand / Eugene Debs with his German ideology / On the great Red Special to the promised land!" (77) Connolly holds various jobs through the schemings, betrayals, and strikes; his wife and eldest daughter meanwhile are desperately sewing shirts to make a little money. At the end he is invited back to Ireland to work with Jim Larkin in establishing the Irish Transport Workers' Union. Lillie understands his need to move on: "To turn the whole world upside-down / Is a task for no fixed citizen of an enclosed and guarded town" (85).

In part 5, Connolly goes to Belfast as Union organizer, founds the Irish Labor Party, and becomes involved with political and social equality for women. The second half of part 5 draws its shape from the rise and fall of the Lockout in Dublin in 1913–14. Despite a ban on all gatherings, a meeting is held in O'Connell Street, and Connolly comments: "It is just that there was this great field full of folk / And all of a sudden they were aware / That all of their lives they had been lined up for war: / And all of a sudden, on Sunday, it had come" (58). He introduces mass picketing, which is overwhelmed by armed scabs. Help is sought from the British trade unions, but the leadership refuses aid, and the Ardens hammer home that this refusal led to the workers' defeat.

Part 6 begins with a Prologue from Irish legend: young King Conaire is bound by three prohibitions from druids, and he breaks all three. The structure of this final section is the progression among the rival Irish movements toward the glory and defeat of the Easter Rising. Connolly struggles to decide whether or not to commit the Citizens' Army to the Rising, then Padraic Pearse inspires him to fight now. The doomed, heroic fight at the Post Office in Dublin occupies the last act; and after Connolly is executed, he is resurrected and concludes:

> When the fire and sword and fury flew
> At them in Russia, China, Cuba, Africa, Vietnam
> And indeed once more in Ireland, my own home,
> They could not credit what it was they'd done,
> Or what it was in Dublin we'd begun
> At Easter nineteen hundred and sixteen—
> We were the first to roll away the stone
> From the leprous wall of the whitened tomb
> We were the first to show the dark deep hole within
> Could be thrown open to the living sun. (106)

The Non-Stop Connolly Show was rehearsed over a three-month period with a largely amateur cast, some playing as many as twenty-five different parts. The Ardens aimed at a democratic and cooperative way of working, but difficulties developed and they acted increasingly as directors (according to Paddy Marsh's account in *Theatre Quarterly*; the Ardens' essay does not mention problems). The *Show* was first presented in Liberty Hall, Dublin, the headquarters of the Irish Transport and General Workers' Union, where several scenes in the last two plays are set, and Connolly's life has, of course, additional meaning in Dublin. The performance began at noon on March 29, 1975 (Easter Saturday) and ended twenty-six hours later. The company subsequently played parts of the *Show* in Dublin and on tour. When the work reached London as *The Non-Stop Connolly Cycle*, it played at the Almost Free Theater. Starting on May Day, 1976, the piece was presented in fourteen parts, with a daily installment at midday. The cast numbered twenty-five, and the *Cycle* was described as "readings with music and songs," with the credits "devised, written and staged" by the Ardens.

While some London critics could not understand why Connolly merited attention, most reviewers enjoyed themselves. *Time Out*'s critic heard "a sometimes convoluted, often inspired, always intriguing and undoubtedly courageous script";[20] and Catherine Itzin had only praise: "The language is lyrical, beautiful; the ironies imaginative, the staging inventive and exciting."[21] Especially, some reviewers were caught up in the energy of the performance; Harold Hobson—often unimpressed by Arden's plays—this time found "a splendid swagger, with terrific Irish proletarian songs that set the feet stamping,"[22] and the *Daily Telegraph* critic thought "the gusto of the writing, the hefty jog-trot of the verse and the roar of the ballads add up to something like a folk epic."[23]

The Non-Stop Connolly Show is indeed massive—longer than *Mourning Becomes Electra* or *Back to Methuselah* and on the scale of Thomas Hardy's *The Dynasts*. The epic, as well as episodic, *Show* takes the amplitude that Arden would have liked for *The Workhouse Donkey* and that he allowed himself in *The Island of the Mighty*. Yet Connolly himself is rarely colorful or exciting, for the Ardens audaciously involve the spectator in committee meetings and in doctrinal disputes. Other playwrights of the Left have written in recent years of their leaders in the past: among them Peter Weiss in *Trotsky in Exile* (1972) and Robert Bold on Lenin in 1917 in *State of Revolution* (1977). In the many songs John McGrath's picture of the Scottish Socialist hero of the same period, John MacLean, *The Game's a Bogey* (1975), is the closest parallel. In requiring an audience interested in problems of Socialist theory, though, Trevor Griffiths' account of Antonio Gramsci in Turin in 1920 in *Occupations* (1970) shows a closer resemblance to the Ardens' *Connolly Show*.

Since the Ardens keep Connolly a representative figure, the audience is shown what he did, rather than told why.

That he was probably quarrelsome and difficult to work with can only be inferred. His periodic returns to domestic life, always to poverty and to the loyal wife, are unilluminating; and the wife and daughter stay shadowy, in contrast to Maud Gonne and Countess Markiewicz, of whom the audience know something outside the plays.

Most of the issues in *The Non-Stop Connolly Show* remain relevant: nationalism and Protestant-Roman Catholic rivalry in Ireland; revolution versus Parliamentary gradualism; the role of trades unions and of middle-class supporters in promoting Socialism. Though some sections (particularly part 4 and the first half of part 5) are flat and relentlessly documentary, the Ardens are painstakingly educating their audiences in an alternative, people's history in which the union leaders, the Socialist theorists, the workers, and the faceless capitalists are in the foreground and in which the generals and prime ministers are in the background. While the rewards of this hugely ambitious drama are mainly intellectual, frequently also the Ardens present striking verse, exuberance and high spirits which recall *The Workhouse Donkey* and *The Little Gray Home.*

Vandaleur's Folly

Vandaleur's Folly, "an Anglo-Irish melodrama," is about the rise and fall of a Socialist cooperative estate at Ralahine, County Clare, in 1831–33. Vandaleur, an idealistic landowner, believed that his "duty was the reform of the rural economy."[24] In Dublin he hears a speech by Robert Owen, preaching the cooperative dream and himself practicing it at New Lanark. Inspired by the speech, Vandaleur brings Craig from England to help him, proclaiming: "No stewards in the co-operative, no middle-men, but a power / From all the people, by election, to control and plan / The work, the wages, and the wealth of Ralahine" (39). Poor tenant farmers become equal in the co-op, a reaping-machine is bought, and the first half ends with a successful harvest.

The Ralahine commune, however, soon has problems. The High Sheriff watches the estate because its members include Micheal, wanted because he killed the corrupt estate steward before the cooperative era. The neighboring absentee landowner, Baker-Fortescue (the name is also that of the landlord in *The Little Gray Home in the West*), mistrusts its success and wants to ride across its cornfields in pursuit of servant girls (which he hunts instead of foxes!). Baker-Fortescue is humiliated in a duel after he has insulted Mrs. Emily Vandaleur: his belt-buckle is hit and his trousers fall down. Baker-Fortescue finally tricks Vandaleur into gambling at the Hell Fire Club in Dublin, and Vandaleur in the end bets the estate and loses. He disappears, and his wife takes over and acts again as a traditional landlord.

Emily and Baker-Fortescue are rivals in the subplot. Baker-Fortescue is engaged in the illegal slave trade, with his trading goods hidden near Ralahine. Roxana comes from America and with Emily, Micheal, and Roisin, Micheal's sister, seeks evidence that will convict Baker-Fortescue and his associate, Wilberforce. In the final confrontation Roisin kills Wilberforce; and Baker-Fortescue, who is involved in a failed Orange-Tory plot to prevent the accession of Queen Victoria, kills himself. Micheal and Roxana, who have fallen in love, succeed in escaping to America, where he will help to form the Fenian Brotherhood. All the events are witnessed and commented on by William Thompson, who is working to establish a similar cooperative but who dies before succeeding, and by Anna Wheeler, his lover and collaborator, and also a pioneer feminist.

The Ardens' lengthy introduction explains that the plot had to be complex because of the "need to interlink a number of political themes (Irish tenants, black slaves, co-operation v. exploitation, co-operation v. sectarian rivalry, revolution v. reform, feminism, racialism, predatory sexuality, and so on, with all their contradictions) against a background of a society at a time of critical change" (xii). They intended the play "as a useful contribution to a better understanding of Anglo-Irish conflict: how reformist advances have continually been set back by aggressive reaction, driving the Irish people again and again to 'terrorist' methods" (ix). Further, with characteristic honesty and seriousness, they list their divergences from historical fact.

Vandaleur's Folly, in eighteen scenes and a Prologue and Epilogue, has thirty characters plus ladies, gentlemen, relatives, peasants, soldiers, and guerillas, yet was presented by nine actors. The play was staged by the 7:84 Company in the fall of 1978, the group who had performed *The Ballygombeen Bequest*. The Ardens directed, and the show toured to Lancaster, Oxford, Belfast, the Dublin Theater Festival, and elsewhere. The Ardens' introduction complains, however, that the actors were insufficiently Socialist and that the posters and leaflets prepared with the aim of aiding audiences in linking the play with the current situation in Northern Ireland were not used.

Because *Vandaleur's Folly* was not played in London, there are few reviews. Comment was mostly negative. Tony Allen and Mary-Ann Lysaght found the heroes, Vandaleur, Micheal, and Roxana "drab, sexless and underwritten." They wrote also that although the subject is Irish, the piece "lacked humour and bawdy; the music and songs were presented, for the most part, without conviction; and the only attempt at dancing was nipped severely in the bud. . . . It lacked, in a word, *Irishness*." Also, the play left out "the internal life of the co-op" and "the poor peasant Irish who were its members," while space was found irrelevantly to praise Thompson and Wheeler.[25] Jeremy Treglown thought the problem with the script was "the over-inclusiveness liable to afflict any historical narrative, particularly one written, like this, within a predetermined ideological framework. . . . [The] narrative unwieldiness is not helped by the additional demand to relate what we are seeing to the current situation in Ireland."[26] Robin Thornber placed the blame on the use of the conventions of melodrama: the issues "deserve to be explored in the honest and direct way of David Hare's *Fanshen*. Instead, D'Arcy and Arden have staged their story as a Victorian melodrama . . . which allows an enthusiastic and accomplished company to camp up some of the hammier passages without being too embarrassed. But it also has the unintentional effect of making the villain, a mad major and hell-raising, crowing and baying Regency buck, the most charismatic character around, if not the most sympathetic."[27]

The play is not wholly successful in providing varied entertainment while pursuing its several didactic aims: the rediscovery of people who have lessons for us; a look at the possibilities of cooperatives; an account of early nineteenth-century Ireland in terms of how this determined current Irish problems; and a perspective on racism, imperialism, and womens' rights at that time. Nevertheless, *Vandaleur's Folly* has more shape and potentially more pace and excitement than much of the *Connolly Show*.

The Ardens have referred to these three—or eight—plays as all part of some massive consideration of Ireland. The plays actually differ considerably. *Vandaleur's Folly* is closest to the style of *The Hero Rises Up*, though this time the Ardens sometimes appear merely dutiful in tracing out the historical ramifications of their story. *The Little Gray Home in the West*, with more limited aims, succeeds as highly entertaining propaganda, mastering this form as "Harold Muggins" failed to do. While the *Connolly Show* is unique, breaking all the conventions of compressions on the stage to incorporate a whole life, the detail risks swamping the portrait of Connolly as a true hero. In this series of plays, apart from theatrical qualities, the Ardens succeed in their aim of giving insights into unusual aspects of Ireland, unfamiliar in terms of both the history books and today's newspapers.

Pearl

Pearl, Arden's third radio play, running two hours (the published text is a little longer), was transmitted by the British Broadcasting Corporation on July 3, 1978. *Pearl* received substantial critical attention, partly because a film of its recording was shown two days earlier on television, on "The South Bank Show." Arden subtitled the work in *Radio Times* as "a play about a play within the play." Set about 1640, *Pearl* begins with a performance of *Julius Caesar*, organized by Lord Grimscar, in a Yorkshire town. Soon the production is broken up by Grip, a fanatical Puritan preacher. In the audience is Pearl, daughter of an Indian and an Irish woman transported to Virginia, widely traveled but newly arrived in England. Excited by the play, she would like to act. She has come on a secret mission to Grimscar, with the message that the Irish Catholics, led by O'Neill, are

ready to rise against King Charles I. Grimscar also fears the
king is growing tyrannical and will suppress Parliament.
Countess Belladonna, Grimscar's mistress and a royalist, is
going to finance his putting on a play in her mansion in London, with women actresses for the first time, and written by
his friend, Backhouse. Backhouse, aided by Pearl, takes the
play from the Old Testament, as "The Brave Deeds of Godly
Queen Esther for the Salvation of her People Israel." This
play, says Pearl, will be "the true voice of the common people."[28] Belladonna, of course, does not want a popular,
Parliamentary play, so the actor Barnabas changes the
emphasis and the title to "The Tragedy of Haman and his
Contentious Rebellion against the Commands of the King of
Persia" (59). Meanwhile, Backhouse and Pearl, who are now
lovers, prepare privately an epilogue to the play to make the
message more explicit: she will be "no longer Queen Esther
dead and buried for thousands of years, but the very spirit
and shape of the most implacable new-fangled enmity to the
Crown and Throne of England" (65). When Backhouse's play
is presented, the designer (a tool of Belladonna) prevents the
planned ending, stabbing Backhouse and delivering his own
pro-monarchy epilogue. Grimscar is discredited, Belladonna
scars and blinds Pearl, and news comes that the Scots have
defeated the king's army. The final episode describes what is
to come: war and suffering in England and Ireland, and also
the consequences for the theater: "From that day to this the
word of the Common People of England, most powerful in
the strength of the Lord, had little or nothing to do with the
word of their tragic poets or the high genius of their actors.
You might say this did small hurt to the body and bones, but
deeper, within the soul" (76).

Most of the language is dignified and timeless, with a few
archaic words such as "paps." Apart from the verse of
Backhouse's play, Arden again turns to verse for high emotional moments and for this enigmatic couplet: "Pearl is
bright and Pearl is dark / We lodge our jewel in the walled
green park" (21).

Peter Porter disliked the language, writing "*Pearl* is built
up of half-timbered Jacobean and extravagant theatre fus-
tian. Characters sonorously pronouncing 'I do most

apprehensively misdoubt . . .'; courtesans speaking of 'the curvatures of my white body'; someone saying of the local lord that 'he has written to enkindle his whore'—such language doesn't only send conviction flying, it brings out the fruity and the over-ripe in actors' performances."[29] Michael Billington, on the other hand, spoke for the majority of reviewers when he described it as "language of Shakespearean richness: concrete, earthy, compact with images and ideas."[30]

For much of the drama, Arden seemed to be showing both sides of the questions raised, as Billington noted:

What is particularly heartening about *Pearl* is that, though it stands for a particular cause (the ideal of a non-sectarian human brotherhood), it has the early sixties Arden gift of challenging its own certainties. For example, the play leads you to endorse the idea that once Parliament is re-established, the King's overweening power will inevitably be diminished. But, just as you are going along with that, a royalist Duchess throws out a subversive remark like: 'Meanwhile the King's enemies at home are diverted by having a Parliament to talk in—and talk to the content of their chattering hearts'. That is vintage Arden: making you emotionally support parliamentary democracy while questioning its ultimate value.[31]

Arden's historical imagination is at work here on a great deal of data; he is less bound by fact than with James Connolly, but far more than when King Arthur was his subject. One difficulty is his expectation of some knowledge of the conflicts preceding the Civil War in England, and of the less familiar history of Ireland at the time—and also of the Bible story Backhouse dramatizes. Arden is engaged by such speculations as what went wrong for Ireland at this time, and whether it might have been averted. He asks why the Parliamentarians, with whom he identifies politically, were against theater. He wonders why theater declined after Shakespeare's time; Backhouse observes: "We spoke once to the whole people. But these days we have rejected the homespun jackets, the square-toed shoes, and the forthright word of the godly tradesmen. And by God they've rejected *us*" (46). Billington identified such period issues as "the futile historical division between the King's common enemies in

the late 1630's" and "the ruinous division between the
language of the common people and that of the dramatists,
that followed the closure of the theatres in 1642."[32] One
might add that good working relationships between authors
and actors are presented in the Caroline theater.

Some critics were titillated by the autobiographical streak:
a dramatist whose work is inspired and altered by a woman,
and "the balancing-point" of a play distorted through
changed "emphasis" (59; like *Island of the Mighty*). Of most
import today is the faith in political purposes in theater.
Billington supplies also "the division in man between his
repressive and Dionysiac urges."[33]

Though Porter found the play "Balzacian in its density of
detail and in the ramifications of the complex plot,"[34] most
critics were impressed, and Billington gushed: "*Pearl* was
beyond price: a radio play of staggering richness. It told a
good, if admittedly complex, story. It was, particularly in
Alfred Bradley's wittily expert production, rooted in the
concrete. And it sent poetic images speeding out of the radio
set like bullets to their target. . . . It belongs right up there
with Arden's richest plays (*Serjeant Musgrave's Dance*, *The
Workhouse Donkey*, *Armstrong's Last Goodnight*) in that it
leaves you with an overpowering image: of division in both
human sensibility and political life."[35]

"Don Quixote"

Arden continued with radio work with a three-hour adaptation of Cervantes' novel, *Don Quixote*, broadcast by the
B.B.C. in two parts, on September 29 and October 6, 1980,
directed by Alfred Bradley. Arden discussed the problems of
adapting such a huge and rambling text in *Radio Times*; the
dialogue, for example: "It's not like Dickens where you can
put it into dramatic speech simply by cutting three sentences
in every four. If one tries to do that the whole rambling baro-
que style disappears into thin air." Arden noted that he had
not been able to do justice to such themes as Cervantes' implicit criticism of his world and the attitude of Spain to
Muslim countries. What really appealed to him about the
book was its "experimenting with different levels of reality

and exploring where fantasy merges with reality. [Cervantes] extends this in an interesting way. In the first part of the book Don Quixote goes off on his travels and his friends and relatives eventually get him back home by entering into his fantasy world and manipulating him through it. If Cervantes had finished it there it wouldn't have been anything like so interesting. . . . Part One was so successful that many pirate editions were sold. It also inspired one of those flashy writers who can knock a book together in a fortnight to write a Part Two. So when Cervantes begins *his* Part Two he sets Don Quixote off into a world where those he meets have already read about him in Part One, where some of them have read the unofficial Part Two, and where others lay claim to acquaintance with a non-existent account. . . . The levels of reality become completely muddled."[36] Thus the production brought to mind the work of Jorge Borges and Laurence Sterne's *Tristram Shandy* as well as remote Spain.

Arden's significant change was including Cervantes in the play. Cervantes is the first character introduced, a tax collector aged fifty-five unjustly imprisoned in La Mancha. Chatting with the local priest, he hears of an old man in the village who read too many romances, which led him into many curious adventures. This man becomes Cervantes' model for Quixote, and we have some sense of the milieu in which Quixote moves.

"Don Quixote" was lavishly praised: "It is marvellously funny, with many complex ironies," wrote Jeremy Brooks,[37] while Geoffrey Cannon asserted that "it is a masterpiece; an indispensable illumination of Cervantes, and of Arden's own vision."[38] Paul Vallely outlined the merits:

Bob Grant's marvellous Quixote . . . was a man living in the past, an Edwardian gentleman who lapsed into Victorian grandiloquence when the mood took him—silly, self-deluding but ultimately not without a pathetic nobility. Bernard Cribbins's Sancho had great depth—a man by turns gullible, shrewd, greedy and comradely, and, above all, superbly funny. . . . The result is vintage Arden: the poetry, of both the ordinary folk and the fantastical knight, is deep, dark and powerful; the canvas is almost Shakespearian in the breadth of his portrait of Cervantes' society and its workings. The sense of theatre is electric and epic, in the Brechtian

sense, in style; the humour and wit range from producing the ur-
bane smile to the belly-laugh; and the themes of anarachy versus
order and the relationship of the individual to society are fruitfully
re-explored.[39]

"Garland for a Hoar Head"

Arden's 1982 radio play, "Garland for a Hoar Head,"
broadcast by the B.B.C. on February 25, examined the early
Tudor poet, John Skelton. Arden explained how, when he
first read Skelton, "I realized I had turned up a poet whom I
could not understand, in the ordinary sense of the word, but
whose very incomprehensibility seemed crystal clear to my
imagination. . . . One was presented with an image of a poet
all alone in the oppressive atmosphere of his sanctuary
house . . . relentlessly and ferociously turning his political
grievances into surrealist verbal gold. . . . There is such contrast through his work but the style is always recognisably
Skelton. . . . He can move from majestic declamation to col-
loquial gutter-abuse or affectionate familiarity or to sudden
sexual arousal in the space of half a line."[40] The 125-minute
play focused on Skelton in old age, in 1522, staying with the
Countess of Surrey in her castle at Sheriff Hutton, Yorkshire,
talking bawdy to the maids while engaging in prolonged
conflict with Cardinal Wolsey. Paula Neuss, reviewing in
the *Times Literary Supplement*, thought Arden excel-
lently showed off the poems in a plausible framework,
or Garland.[41]

Chapter Ten
Conclusion

Great claims have been made for John Arden. Jack Richardson noted that he was "considered by many close to the theater to be England's best contemporary playwright," while D. A. N. Jones described him as "the only dramatic poet in English, outside Nigeria."[1] Albert Hunt called him "one of the greatest dramatists in the English language for several centuries," and Adrian Mitchell even claimed that "he is the greatest British playwright since Shakespeare."[2] Arden, on the other hand, has never had a Broadway nor Shaftesbury Avenue production, and his reputation appears to have declined in the 1970s.

Various reasons for Arden's lack of wide popularity can be listed: he has confused commentators by his unpredictability; his interest in verse and in dignified speech has been unfashionable since the early 1950s; some productions of his plays were feeble. Many of the plays are complex, idiosyncratic, and difficult to grasp at a single hearing. He expects an alert audience willing to follow where an original mind leads. He has been reluctant to meet the requirements of the professional theater, writing for big casts at inordinate length. Other reasons are more fortuitous: accidents of geography, of political gestures, of personality conflicts around real or imagined slights, or refusal to seek worldly commercial success. Arden often seems to have been writing in the wrong era, to date somehow always out of step with audiences and their expectations.

Whatever the explanations, Arden has failed to find a substantial audience. His turning away from the London theater is mainly due to his wish to work with small communities, but is also partly due to the way in which the West End has never turned to him. The inability to find big audiences is especially sad for a man who wants to reach the people in the manner of nineteenth-century melodrama or early twentieth-century music-hall clowning.

Arden is essentially a man of the theater, though readily trying out radio and television. He has acted himself in *The Business of Good Government, The Royal Pardon,* "Harold Muggins," and *The Connolly Show* and likes to direct or to be involved in rehearsals. A whole play, *The Royal Pardon,* explores the balance between reality and make-believe that is the essence of theater. Ideally, he would involve his audience in an exciting neo-Dionysian ritual; instead, he seeks the participation of as many as possible of the people in Kirkbymoorside, Beaford, County Galway, or the streets around Unity Theater. Like Shaw or Brecht, Arden wants his audiences to react to serious issues, but he desires also to entertain them in as many ways as possible: with many characters, colorfully dressed; with striking visual effects, like the besieged house at the end of *Pigs* or the marketplace *coup de théâtre* in *Musgrave;* and with songs and lyrical flights of fancy.

Twelve of the plays are jointly attributed to Margaretta D'Arcy: *The Happy Haven, The Business of Good Government, Ars Longa,* and nearly all the plays since *Left-Handed Liberty* in 1965: *Friday's Hiding, The Royal Pardon,* "Harold Muggins," *The Hero Rises Up, The Little Gray Home in the West,* "Keep Those People Moving!," *The Island of the Mighty, The Non-Stop Connolly Show,* and *Vandaleur's Folly.* Only in *The Little Gray Home in the West* is more than half of it attributed to her; in the other cases, she contributed usually less than half. As she has published nothing that is wholly her own, the reader can only speculate about her role, but Arden has admitted that she is more of a political activist than he is. For *Ars Longa,* according to Arden, she suggested using "the peculiar directness and spontaneous development of 'classical conventions'" of children's improvisations.[3] She seems responsible for broad effects and unsubtle characterizations in *The Royal Pardon,* "Harold Muggins," *The Hero Rises Up,* and "Keep Those People Moving!" She is likely to be responsible also for the acting style required for *The Little Gray Home in the West;*

for scripts that are intended as starting points for actors, *Ars Longa* and "Harold Muggins"; and for *The Hero Rises Up* as "a play which need not be *done properly*."

The range of Arden's language has been sufficiently illustrated already: in both prose and verse he displays simplicity, beauty, dignity, rightness. He is so accomplished in this respect from the start that he shows off Irish, West Indian, and East European speech in *The Waters of Babylon*, while the sixteenth-century Scots of *Armstrong* and the seventeenth-century echoes of *Pearl* are a tour de force.

Frank Cox has commented that "when he writes of the fanatical Musgrave and the saddened Attercliffe, of Annie and her malformed baby under the ground, or of Sailor Sawney and Daffodil, the crazy Old Croaker tearing up the washing and Blackmouth howling at the moon, these characters seem worth a score of Jimmy Porters, Archie Rices, Beatie Bryants and Sarah Kahns, for they haunt the mind as none of these latter do as the products of a poetic intelligence."[4] True, but the distinction is in more than creating characters: Arden creates an underworld of feeling, recalls the spirit of the past, and presents the essential human values found in the finest ballads. His is a mastery of communicating the essence of groups, rather than of individuals: the unity and disunity within Musgrave's band, the Sawneys together against the world, and the loyalties of Armstrong's clan, confused by a changing world.

The difficulties in Arden's plays can be exaggerated. Some of the plays—notably *Musgrave*, *Armstrong*, and *The Island of the Mighty*—become more comprehensible at second seeing or reading; but on the other hand *Live Like Pigs* or *The Happy Haven* are readily accessible. Sometimes characters behave in confusing ways: Musgrave's attitudes are admirable while his actions are not; Krank and Butterthwaite are likeable people whose behavior is questioned, yet, as Arden has said, "the likeable rogue is a very old convention." At times, too, one is bewildered about what to think. Arden deliberately bewilders his audience through most of *Musgrave* because he himself is questioning the pacifist position, but at other times his subtle intelligence may have created more uncertainty than he intended. Without his statement in a letter that "Lindsay was wrong" in *Armstrong* and in an interview that Butterthwaite's corruption does a "great deal less harm" than Feng's integrity in *The Workhouse Donkey*, few would feel absolutely sure of the author's intent.

Nearly all these difficulties fall into place, however, after the recurring theme has been grasped—that of authority and the place of the rare, free, vital, spontaneous man in modern, ordered societies. Authority rests in social institutions: kings and clergy in the past; police and mayors today. Authority is naval discipline in "The Life of Man"; Caligula, the incorruptible councillor; the housing official and policeman in *Pigs*; mayor, parson, constable, and dragoon officer in *Musgrave*; the doctor in *The Happy Haven*; Herod; the routine and regular hours of the architect's office in *Wet Fish*; police and government in *The Workhouse Donkey*; the Bishop of Bamberg and the Emperor against Ironhand; the king and Lindsay against Armstrong; King John in *Liberty*; kings and the constable in *The Royal Pardon*; soldiers, kings, and ministers in *The Bagman*; Arthur, Strathclyde, and Gododdin in *The Island*; and Grabitall and the Employers in *The Connolly Show*. Individuals without office take authority on themselves, like Henry Ginger in *Babylon*, the Bargee in *Musgrave*, and Baker-Fortescue in *The Little Gray Home in the West*. Arden knows the complexity of authority and that the police, the Labor councillors, and the Conservative businessmen somehow share it. Levels of authority are often considered: the protagonist of *Soldier, Soldier* must leave to meet his obligations; the dragoons come from outside to seize Musgrave; Doctor Copperthwaite is variously responsible to the mayor, wealthy benefactors, and the Ministry of Health; the Home Secretary in London could intervene in Butterthwaite's borough; the program for *Armstrong* contained a chart of hierarchies of responsibility. Sometimes authority figures are detestable, like the Headmaster in *Ars Longa* and the constable in *The Royal Pardon*; but Arden usually evinces understanding of the men who attempt to provide good government. He is kindly to Feng in *The Workhouse Donkey*, writes almost an apologia for Herod, and did not make clear his disapproval of Lindsay to many who saw *Armstrong*. As a result, misunderstanding exists and he is accused of amorality or of lacking a view of his own.[5]

While Arden may be fair to authority, he prefers the rebel, who is often faulty or unprincipled by conventional moral standards. These rebels begin with Jones in "The Life of Man," who will not work, and they continue with Krank, the Sawneys, Sparky and Annie, the old people in *The Happy Haven*, Joseph and Mary, the Art Master's wife, the actors and soldier in *The Royal Pardon*, the Young Woman of *The Bagman*, Padraic, the Wild Cat Picts, Connolly, and Pearl. The would-be rebel is sometimes an authority figure himself, like the Scottish private in *Solider, Soldier,* Musgrave, Alderman Butterthwaite of *The Workhouse Donkey*, Ironhand, Armstrong, King John, Nelson, and Vandaleur. The Scots soldier moves on after his petty success and Nelson continues winning battles, but the others are defeated, all by higher authority except King John, whose downfall is best attributable to bad luck.

Other conflicts between authority and the rebel are resolved in different ways. Krank in *Wet Fish*, Joseph and Mary, and the Art Master's wife triumph, as do the old people in *The Happy Haven* and the actors of *The Royal Pardon* in more fairy-tale settings. Other rebels are defeated; Krank in *Babylon*, Ironhand, Armstrong, King John, and Connolly all die. Padraic in *The Little Grey Home* dies and comes to life again; Pearl is blinded. Jones in "The Life of Man" may have drowned, but this is not certain; and, while Butterthwaite in *Donkey* is crushed, he survives to fight again. Vandaleur vanishes; the laborers in *Friday's Hiding*, too, lose, but will resume the battle on the next Friday. Even if the rebel fails, authority may lose as well: Anthract and his henchmen in "The Life of Man" are drowned, Weislingen is poisoned, Doctor Copperthwaite changed to a small child, and Arthur is killed, as is Baker-Fortescue in *The Little Gray Home*. The conflicts in Arden and for his dream characters in *The Bagman* continue, as does the Irish struggle in *The Little Gray Home in the West*.

This analysis suggests that the plays often end with an action that is conclusive but hard to judge. Whether the outcome is trival (the soldier leaves the Scuffhams' household; Krank leaves the architect's office) or of national importance (the deaths of Armstrong, King John, and King Arthur), the consequence usually is *probably* good. In the majority of cases the rebels lose, but this loss is qualified by an affirmative hint: whether Jones of "The Life of Man" is dead or not, his few days on the ship are remembered; Cassidy, Butterthwaite, and others will continue the Krank spirit, just as Col and Rachel will maintain the Sawney spirit; Musgrave, Attercliffe, and Connolly may plant a whole orchard through their deaths; Lindsay learns that he achieves damnation in deceiving Armstrong; Magna Carta—its best points contributed by King John—will survive though the king dies. While a commonplace, dreary, occasionally unscrupulous society is likely to dominate, in Arden's society a hundred flowers may bloom and challenge uniformity. Few are wholly bad (like the Bargee and Blomax in *The Donkey*, who are unharmed); the others may fail or be deposed, but more people resembling them will appear. However much is wrong with authority, free spirits continue.

At times, Arden concedes the need for order and good government, while wanting no part himself in administering it; at other times, he dreams of a society where no government is needed. Because he identifies so fully with the rebels, they are often made to behave outrageously in order to force consideration of the rights of the rebel (Armstrong and Ironhand, and to a lesser degree Krank and Butterthwaite). Arden enjoys the Sawneys, and he pleads for them in a world that seems to have been made safe only for Jacksons.

The Jacksons represent a group seen only rarely in Arden's dramas, the ordinary people. Like the Scuffhams in *Soldier, Soldier*, Ruth and the Treddle-hoyles in *Wet Fish*, and the poor in *The Hero Rises Up*, *The Island of the Mighty*, and *The Little Gray Home in the West*, they are born victims. The miners are inadequate when Musgrave challenges them, and the sailors in "The Life of Man" respond to Jones too late. Perhaps the best is Mrs. Hitchcock, with the milk of human kindness beneath the no-nonsense, North-country manner. Mrs. Hitchcock is one of several tough, efficient, worldly wise women, with the inn hostess in *Good Government*,

Rachel Sawney, Eleanor of Aquitaine, the farmer's sister in *Friday's Hiding*, and Mrs. Connolly.

The commonest type of woman in the plays, however, is not a leader in public matters; she is nevertheless free and spontaneous and a worthy companion for the rebels. These women, unless young, are usually promiscuous, and the line includes Mary in *Soldier, Soldier,* Gloria and Wellesley in *The Donkey*, the Art Master's wife in *Ars Longa*, Adelheid in *Ironhand*, Lindsay's mistress in *Armstrong*, Lady De Vesci in *Liberty*, Esmeralda in *The Royal Pardon*, the woman in *Squire Jonathan*, Nelson's Emma, Arthur's Gwenhwyvar, and Pearl. When the women are at a lower social level, they are golden-hearted whores, like Bones's girl, Sparky's Annie, and Teresa and Bathsheba in *Babylon*. Most often, whatever the period of action, they have a great deal of liberty and are the equal partners of their menfolk. Their hands very rarely rock cradles, but they often entice and unsettle men and so influence the ruling of the world.

Many of the plays allude to change from a free world to a more rigidly structured one, that has increased emphasis on conformity. Several deal directly with the past, with periods and types of men who may have represented change from past ways to modern ones. Plays set in the present also look back: *Wet Fish* shows the nature of the small store as altering between the 1930s and 1960s, and *Live Like Pigs* examines modern descendants of Elizabethan sturdy beggars. The use of traditional ballads and recognizable older literary forms (Jonson in *Babylon* and *The Workhouse Donkey*; *commedia dell'arte* in *The Happy Haven*; melodrama several times) help to establish the idea of change *and* of tradition.

Neither the past nor scrutiny of the present gave Arden a viable morality or a settled social philosophy,[6] and his own uncertainty explains why his earlier plays have often been found so puzzling. By 1970 he had presented much in the realm of ideas, both his wide vision about freedom, expediency, and authority and his specific comments about such subjects as Cyprus, Vietnam, pacifism, and old people. His failure to achieve a settled world view related to the varied types and contexts of his plays, for his career has been a restless search for the right kind of stage, the right company, the right community. Possibly too much of the concept of a play remains in Arden's mind and is never sufficiently on paper for others to grasp—or perhaps the failing is rather in the organization of theater, that there is never enough time to evolve an absolutely finished Arden play. His intellectuality, which can overcome theatrical qualities, may be his biggest disadvantage as a playwright. In striving to reconcile diverse influences, in seeking to reach a wide public, in exploring the use of verse, song, and music, and in trying to fit in every relevant scene, his work is too often indigestible.

In 1971 Arden announced his conversion to a Marxist world view in the Preface to *Two Autobiographical Plays*. He confirmed this in 1977 in *To Present the Pretence*: "Twelve years ago I looked on at people's struggles, and wrote about them for the stage, sympathetically but as an onlooker. Without consciously intending it, I have become a participant. . . . I write from henceforth in that capacity."[7] The obvious reasons for his descent from the fence on the Lefthand side are his observations in India, the outbreak of violent conflict in Northern Ireland, and the influence of D'Arcy. His newfound perspective influenced the final layer he and D'Arcy added to *The Island of the Mighty* and determined the subject and viewpoint of *The Little Gray Home in the West*, *The Non-Stop Connolly Show*, and, to a lesser degree, *Vandaleur's Folly*. Critics since 1971 have too readily accepted the Preface as the complete and final truth about Arden's politics. In fact, in 1977 Arden insisted: "Someone wrote about me recently that I was now a dedicated Communist devoted to violence, which is not true. Nor am I a Maoist revolutionary although through having been in India I have more understanding of revolutionaries and much stronger reservations about the value of pacifism." He continued with the cautious statement: "I think the world is polarising and it is the function of a writer to elucidate what is going on."[8] In the three most recent plays, *Pearl*, "Don Quixote," and "Garland for a Hoar Head," Arden the historian and Arden the poet are again as important as Arden the politician.

What are Arden's strengths? He has a flair for language, especially for the harsh, laconic, Anglo-Saxon-rooted verse line. He is endlessly curious, so that a lively and intelligent mind is always to be perceived in the plays. He has a powerful sense of the past in an age when historical drama is uncommon, re-creating the times of men like Armstrong and King Arthur and, more playfully, Nelson. The stagecraft, the gift for the theatrical moment, provides the shock of the skeleton hoisted as Musgrave dances and many more, such as the apotheosis of Butterthwaite at the end of *The Workhouse Donkey*. Arden has the ambition and audacity to keep attempting something new, trying out length and brevity, mime and masks, music and melodrama, work with and for children. And a good production of an Arden play is not only intellectually satisfying but exuberantly entertaining, promoting good feeling and high spirits, even on such unpromising topics as municipal politics and Irish oppression.

The successes are there to be read, foremost among them *Musgrave*, where mythic imagination best fuses with passionate purpose. *The Waters of Babylon*, *Live Like Pigs*, and, especially, *The Workhouse Donkey* overflow with energy and vitality. Other pieces are limited in size and scope: the spiky, abruptly episodic *Ars Longa*; the gentler, more relaxed *Royal Pardon*; the dream-nightmare meditation, *The Bagman*. In contrast *Armstrong's Last Goodnight* has a multiplicity of character and incident, and a breadth equalled only by Brecht in modern times. Arden still awaits full recognition of his great and varied achievements—and is still writing.

Notes and References

Preface

1. Arden, *Plays One* (London, 1977), p. 6.
2. Ibid., pp. 7–8.

Chapter One

1. "Building the Play" (interview), *The New British Drama,* ed. Henry Popkin (New York, 1964), p. 582. The biographical information in this section, including all the direct quotations, comes from the above and three other sources: "A Thoroughly Romantic View," *London Magazine* 7 (July 1960): 11–13; "Who's for a Revolution?," *Tulane Drama Review*, no. 34 (Winter 1966), pp. 41–42, 46; and Ira Peck, "Art, Politics and John Arden," *New York Times,* April 10, 1966, Sec. 2, pp. 1, 3.
2. Quoted by Albert Hunt, "Anarchy in Yorkshire," *Peace News*, August 23, 1963, p. 1.
3. Harold Clurman, *The Naked Image* (New York: Macmillan, 1966), pp. 200–201.
4. Harold Hobson, "One Up from the Gorillas," *Sunday Times* (London), July 11, 1965, p. 35.
5. Anon., "Four Authors in Search of a Play," *Times* (London), June 23, 1967, p. 10.
6. Arden describes the event in *To Present the Pretence* (London, 1977), pp. 46–48, 51–60, and Victoria Manchester comments in "Let's Do Some More Undressing," *Educational Theatre Journal* 19 (Dec. 1967):502–10.
7. Catherine Itzin lists the Ardens' community theater work in the Chronology in her *Stages in the Revolution* (London, 1980), pp. 369–87.

Chapter Two

1. John Russell Taylor, *Anger and After*, (London, rev. ed., 1969), p. 86.
2. Gillian Reynolds, "Oldies but Goodies," *Guardian*, April 17, 1971, p. 8.
3. Francis Dillon, "Fossicking," *Listener* 84 (July 22, 1971):123.

4. *The Waters of Babylon* in *Three Plays* (Harmondsworth, 1964); hereafter page references cited in parentheses in the text are to this edition.
5. Kenneth Tynan, "The Ego Triumphant," *Observer*, Oct. 27, 1957, p. 17.
6. Julius Novick, *Beyond Broadway* (New York: Hill & Wang, 1968), p. 52.
7. Robert Pasolli, "Theater," *Nation* 202 (May 1, 1967): 574.
8. Introduction to *Three Plays*, p. 10.
9. The second phrase is from "A Thoroughly Romantic View," *London Magazine* 7 (July 1960):14. The first and third remarks are from my interview.
10. Simon Trussler, "Building the Play," in *New British Drama*, p. 590.
11. "The Book of the Play," *Tribune*, Feb. 5, 1965, p. 14.
12. "Who's for a Revolution?" *Tulane Drama Review*, no. 34 (Winter, 1966), p. 46.
13. "A Thoroughly Romantic View," p. 14.
14. "Arden of Chichester," *Plays and Players* 10 (Aug., 1963): 17.
15. *Live Like Pigs* in *Three Plays* (Harmondsworth, 1964); hereafter page references cited in parentheses in the text are to this edition.
16. Laurence Kitchin, *Mid-Century Drama* (London: Faber, rev. ed., 1962), p. 118.
17. T.C. Worsley, "Pigs and Peacocks," *New Statesman* 56 (Oct. 11, 1958): 486.
18. "Arden's Unsteady Ground," *Modern British Dramatists*, ed. John Russell Brown (Englewood Cliffs, N.J.: Prentice-Hall, 1968), p. 111.
19. Henry Hewes, "Here's Mud in Your Sty!" *Saturday Review* 48 (June 26, 1965):41.
20. "Arden," *Nation* 200 (June 21, 1965): 681–682.
21. Ronald Hayman, *John Arden* (London, 1969), pp. 14, 15, 17, 18.
22. P.H. "*Live Like Pigs* at Theatre Upstairs," *Stage,* Feb. 17, 1972, p. 20; Nigel Andrews, "*Live Like Pigs,*" *Plays and Players* 19 (Apr. 1972): 49; Derek Mahon, "The Good Life," *Listener* 85 (Feb. 17, 1972), p. 224; Harold Hobson, "Brothers-in-Arms," *Sunday Times*, Feb. 13, 1972, p. 29.
23. Richard Findlater, *"Live Like Pigs," The Encore Reader,* ed. Charles Marowitz *et al.* (London: Methuen, 1965), p. 93.
24. Hayman, *John Arden*, p. 15.
25. "Building the Play," p. 585.

26. Anon.; *"Like Pigs* Play Stirs a Town," *Yorkshire Evening Post*, Oct. 3, 1958.
27. Anon; "Civic Visit to *Live Like Pigs," Yorkshire Evening Post*, Oct. 9, 1958.
28. "Who's for a Revolution?" p. 44.
29. Worsley, "Pigs and Peacocks," p. 486.
30. Introduction to *Three Plays*, pp. 11, 13.
31. Kenneth Tynan, "A World Fit for Eros," *Observer*, Oct. 5, 1958, p. 19.
32. Findlater, *"Live Like Pigs,"* in *The Encore Reader*, p. 93.
33. George Wellwarth, *The Theater of Protest and Paradox* (New York: New York University Press, 1964), p. 271.
34. *Soldier, Soldier, and Other Plays* (London, 1967); hereafter page references cited in parentheses in the text are to this edition.
35. "Writers and Television: The Writer's View" (interview with Alan Lovell), *Contrast* (London), 2 (Winter, 1962): 125.
36. Ibid., p. 133.
37. Ibid., pp. 132, 133.
38. "Delusions of Grandeur," *Twentieth Century* 169 (Feb., 1961): 205, 204.
39. Irving Wardle, "Jungle of Arden," *Listener* 63 (Feb. 25, 1960): 363.
40. *Soldier, Soldier, and Other Plays* (London, 1967); hereafter page references in parentheses in the text are to this edition.
41. Frederick Laws, "Fashion Leaves Mayfair," *Listener* 66 (Sept. 21, 1961): 442.
42. Angus Wilson, "Long-Distance Perspective," *Observer*, Sept. 10, 1961, p. 22.

Chapter Three

1. *Serjeant Musgrave's Dance* (New York, 1962), p. 6; hereafter page references cited in parentheses in the text are to this edition.
2. "Building the Play," p. 594.
3. Harold Hobson, "Hardly a Silver Lining," *Sunday Times*, Oct. 25, 1959, p. 25.
4. Eric Keown, "At the Play," *Punch* 237 (Oct. 28, 1959): 380.
5. Wellwarth, *Theater of Protest and Paradox*, p. 270.
6. Hilary Spurling, "Royal Fortress," *Spectator*, Dec. 17, 1965, 809–10.
7. "Pacifist Manifesto," *Time*, Mar. 18, 1966, p. 80.

8. Martin Esslin, "Murder of *Musgrave*," *Plays & Players* 13 (Feb. 1966):23.
9. Lindsay Anderson, quoted by Alan Pryce-Jones, "Return to Arden," *Observer*, Nov. 1, 1959, p. 23.
10. John Osborne, leaflet entitled *"Serjeant Musgrave's Dance*: What Kind of a Theatre?"*: issued by Royal Court Theater, November 1959.
11. "Telling a True Tale," *Encore Reader*, p. 128.
12. "Who's for a Revolution?" p. 42.
13. Harold Hobson, "The Pursuit of Happiness," *Sunday Times*, Nov. 8, 1959, p. 25.
14. Albert Bermel, "Racine Uprooted, Arden Transplanted," *New Leader* 51 (Mar. 28, 1966):32.
15. "Building the Play," p. 584.
16. Ibid., pp. 599–600.
17. Other noteworthy alterations in the prompt copy are reducing Musgrave's efforts to build a relationship with Walsh and the three colliers on stage from the start of the marketplace scene (almost eliminating the Bargee's function of interpreting offstage noises). Numerous deletions shorten the play, so that such colorful lines as "Any smart squaddy can carry it away like a tuppenny-ha' penny jam jar" (81) are lost. Otherwise, the copy shows small changes to meet the requirements of the Lord Chamberlain, interjections in some long speeches, and tiny additions (such as "Now put it back" when Sparky shows Annie the card trick in II.1).
18. "Writers and Television," p. 132.
19. Ronald Bryden, "Deep as England," *The Unfinished Hero* (London: Faber, 1969), p. 99.
20. Hilary Spurling, "Royal Fortress," p. 810.
21. Two essays focus on the Bargee's role: Grant Edgar McMillan, "The Bargee in *Serjeant Musgrave's Dance*," *Educational Theatre Journal* 25 (Dec. 1973):500–3, and Barry Thorne *"Serjeant Musgrave's Dance*: Form and Meaning," *Queen's Quarterly* 78 (Winter 1971):567–71.
22. "Building the Play," p. 603.
23. The effect of this moment—when the Bargee's actions parody Musgrave's—is discussed by Albert Hunt in "Arden's Stagecraft," *Modern British Dramatists*, ed. John Russell Brown, pp. 98–99.
24. Richard Gilman, "Arden's Unsteady Ground," *Modern British Dramatists*, p. 112.
25. The point is made by Irving Wardle, "Vision of Judgement," *Encore,* no. 24, (Jan.–Feb. 1960) p. 41.
26. Thomas P. Adler argues that the skeleton's dance is "obviously

a grotesque parody" of the Crucifixion and "a perversion of its essential meaning" in "Religious Ritual in John Arden's *Serjeant Musgrave's Dance,*" *Modern Drama* 16 (Sept. 1973):163.

27. Mary B. O'Connell focuses on the celebration of Spring's approach in suggesting *Musgrave* is shaped by the Mummers Play of Plough Monday, "Ritual Elements in John Arden's *Serjeant Musgrave's Dance,*" *Modern Drama* 13 (Feb. 1971): 356–59.

28. Harold Hobson, "The Soldier's Tale," *Sunday Times,* Dec. 12, 1965, p. 41. Six years after the first hostile review, Hobson admired the play.

29. "Building the Play," p. 593.

30. Jack Richardson, "Musgrave's Dance and Azdak's Circle," *Commentary* 41 (June, 1966):75.

31. "Arden of Chichester," *Plays and Players* 10 (Aug., 1963): 18.

32. "Building the Play," p. 586.

33. Ibid., p. 593.

34. "Programme 3," Royal Court Theater, p. 13. In the 1965–66 season Royal Court productions played in repertory, and *Musgrave* is included in Programs 2, 3, and 4.

35. In interview with Ronald Hayman, "Art Values," *Listener* 104, (Sept. 4, 1980):303.

36. Mentioned in my interview with Arden and in "Building the Play," p. 586. See the full source study: Malcolm Page, "Some Sources of Arden's *Serjeant Musgrave's Dance,*" *Moderna Språk* 67 (1973):332–41.

37. Ira Peck, "Art, Politics and Arden," *New York Times,* Apr. 10, 1966, Sec. 2, p. 3.

38. Ibid.

39. Alan Brien, "Disease of Violence," *Spectator,* Oct. 30, 1959, p. 594.

40. "Building the Play," p. 604.

41. Stuart Hall, *"Serjeant Musgrave's Dance,"* *New Left Review,* no. 1 (Jan.–Feb. 1960), p. 51.

42. David Rush, "Grief, But Good Order," *Moderna Språk* 58 (1964): 454, 458.

43. "Building the Play," p. 590.

44. "Verse in the Theatre," *New Theatre Magazine* 2 (Apr., 1961):14.

Chapter Four

1. "Building the Play," pp. 586–87.

2. *The Happy Haven* in *Three Plays* (Harmondsworth, 1964), p. 198; hereafter page references cited in parentheses in the text

are to this edition. *The Happy Haven* was first published in 1962 in *New English Dramatists*, 4 (Harmondsworth). The earlier edition divides the play into two acts. In the later edition, Act II, Scene 1, is divided into two parts, which become Act II, Scene 5, and Act III, Scene 1. The three-act division was selected presumably because this was the most usual form in the theater.

3. Interview with the writer.
4. William Gaskill, "Comic Masks and *The Happy Haven*," *Encore*, no. 23 (Nov.–Dec., 1960), p. 18.
5. This paragraph is indebted to Irving Wardle, "Live Like Guinea Pigs," *Encore*, no. 28 (Nov.–Dec., 1960), p. 37.
6. See, for example, Kenneth Tynan, *Tynan Right and Left*, (New York, 1967), p. 21; Jeremy Brooks, "Most Likely to Succeed," *New Statesman* 60 (Sept. 24, 1960): 430; and Richard Gilman, "Arden's Unsteady Ground," *Modern British Dramatists*, p. 109.
7. In the 1964 reprint Arden adds to the introduction the suggeston that the attendants can be without masks in the non-clinical scenes, which would destroy this point.
8. Quoted by John Russell Taylor in his introduction to *Three Plays*, p. 13.
9. "Building the Play," p. 587.
10. Frederick Lumley, *New Trends in 20th Century Drama* (London: Barrie & Rockliff, rev. ed., 1967), p. 263.
11. Robert Hatch, "A Coming Talent Casts its Shadow Before," *Horizon* 4 (July, 1962):93–94.
12. "Building the Play," p. 597.
13. *The Workhouse Donkey* (London, 1964), p. 21; hereafter page references cited in parentheses in the text are to this edition.
14. "Arden of Chichester," p. 17.
15. Ibid., p. 18.
16. Bamber Gascoigne, "The Scandals of Arden's Borough," *Observer*, July 14, 1963, p. 26.
17. Alan Seymour, "Chichester '63," *London Magazine* 3 (Sept. 1963):69.
18. Philip French, "Led by Donkeys," *New Statesman* 74 (Nov. 3, 1967):610.
19. Charles Marowitz, *"The Workhouse Donkey," Confessions of a Counterfeit Critic* (London: Eyre Methuen, 1973), pp. 70–71.
20. "Who's for a Revolution?" p. 49.
21. "Arden of Chichester," p. 18.
22. Albert Hunt, "Go to Chichester!" *Peace News*, July 19, 1963, p. 9.

23. Interview with Stuart Burge, BBC radio, July 12, 1967.
24. "On Comedy," *Encore*, no. 57 (Sept.–Oct. 1965), p. 15.
25. "Arden of Chichester," p. 16.
26. "On Comedy," p. 15.
27. Mervyn Jones, "Scandal on the Council," *Tribune*, July 12, 1963, p. 10.
28. "Who's for a Revolution?" p. 49.
29. "On Comedy," p. 14. J.D. Hainsworth notes also a reference to the parable of the unclean spirit driven out only to return with more of his kind, in Luke 11:24–26 ("John Arden and the Absurd," *Review of English Literature* 7 (Oct., 1966):49.
30. "Who's for a Revolution?" pp. 50–51. The commission was in fact for a play suitable for performance by 14 to 17 year-olds.
31. *Ars Longa, Vita Brevis, Encore*, no. 48 (Mar.–Apr., 1964), p. 15.
32. Albert Hunt and Geoffrey Reeves, "Arden: Professionals and Amateurs" (a conversation), *Encore*, no. 57 (Sept.–Oct., 1965), p. 28. Hunt also writes well on *Ars Longa* in his book *Arden: A Study of His Plays* (London, 1974), pp. 115–9, 168–70.
33. Ibid., p. 34.

Chapter Five

1. *Ironhand* (London, 1965), p. 115; hereafter page references cited in parentheses in the text are to this edition.
2. "Building the Play," p. 603.
3. Wallace Fowlie, *Dionysus in Paris* (New York: Meridian Books, 1960), p. 179.
4. *Theatre at Work*, ed. Charles Marowitz and Simon Trussler (London: Methuen, 1967), p. 50; hereafter cited as *Theatre at Work*.
5. *Götz von Berlichingen*, transl. Charles E. Passage (New York: Frederick Ungar, 1965).
6. *Theatre at Work*, p. 50.
7. "Who's for a Revolution?" p. 50.
8. *Armstrong's Last Goodnight* (London, 1965), p. 48; hereafter page references cited in parentheses in the text are to this edition.
9. Quoted by Benedict Nightingale, "The Theatre of Bewilderment," *Guardian*, July 6, 1965, p. 7.
10. Edwin Morgan, *"Armstrong's Last Goodnight,"* *Encore*, no. 50 (July–Aug., 1964), pp. 50–51.
11. Lindsay continues that their deed will not be forgotten for

many years, but here he seems to refer to Armstrong's future fame through ballads.

12. "Letters," *Encore*, no. 51 (Sept.–Oct., 1964), pp. 51, 52.
13. "Who's for a Revolution?" p. 50.
14. National Theater program note.
15. Richard Gilman, "Arden's Unsteady Ground," in *Modern British Dramatists*, p. 114.
16. Ronald Bryden, "Ballad Country," *New Statesman* 67 (May 15, 1964): 783.
17. Mervyn Jones, "Big Fish in a Small Pond," *Tribune*, July 16, 1965, p. 15.
18. "Producing Arden: An Interview with William Gaskill," *Encore*, no. 57 (Sept.–Oct. 1965), p. 23.
19. John Gross, "Rebels and Renegades," *Encounter* 25 (Oct., 1965): 41.
20. *The English and Scottish Popular Ballads*, ed. Francis James Child, (Boston and New York: Houghton-Mifflin, 1889), pp. 362–72; *The Roxburghe Ballads*, ed. J. Woodfall Ebsworth, VI, Pt. 3 (Hertford: Stephen Austin for Ballad Society, 1888), 600–6. Also Madge Elder, *Ballad Country: The Scottish Border* (Edinburgh and London: Oliver & Boyd, 1963), pp. 18–26. "Armstrong's Last Goodnight" is the title of a later ballad, which originally referred to a different Armstrong, executed 70 years later.
21. "Who's for a Revolution?" p. 50.
22. "Questions of Expediency," *Plays and Players* 12 (July 1965):14.
23. Penelope Gilliatt, "Adjusting the Focus of History," *Observer*, July 11, 1965, p. 21. William Gaskill reports that in directing he intended certain effects of "Westerns" and of Japanese movies ("Producing Arden," p. 24).
24. George MacDonald Fraser, *The Steel Bonnets* (London: Barrie & Jenkins, 1971), pp. 227–39. Fraser gives a great deal of interesting background on the Border raiders and their way of life, and useful maps.
25. Conor Cruise O'Brien, *To Katanga and Back* (New York: Simon & Schuster, 1962). O'Brien has himself written a play, *Murderous Angels*, based on his Congo experiences, relating the deaths of Lumumba and Hammarskjold. (Boston: Little, Brown & Co., 1968).
26. National Theater program.
27. "Questions of Expediency," p. 14.
28. "Arden talks about his way of writing plays, to Irving Wardle," *Observer*, June 30, 1963, p. 19.

29. Bamber Gascoigne, "Arden's Border Manoeuvres," *Observer*, May 10, 1964, p. 24.
30. Harold Hobson, "One up from the Gorillas," *Sunday Times* (London), July 11, 1965, p. 35.
31. Ronald Bryden, 'Ballad Country," p. 783.
32. Tom Milne, *"Armstrong's Last Goodnight,"* *Encore*, no. 57 (Sept.–Oct., 1965), p. 37.
33. "Who's for a Revolution?" p. 50.
34. For example, Queen Eleanor is barely mentioned after her major role in the first scene; a barons' council to supervise the king is debated at length, but it is not clear whether it was ever established; the Archbishop leaves on a mission to the Pope in act 3, scene 1, but the outcome is not given; John in the penultimate scene belatedly tries to explain the play's attitude to chivalry in terms of paragraph 54 of the Charter, which has not previously been mentioned.
35. *Theatre at Work*, p. 55.
36. Michael Kustow, *"Left-Handed Liberty,"* *Encore* no. 56 (July–Aug. 1965), p. 39.
37. Penelope Gilliatt, "Plantaganets and Philistines," *Observer*, June 20, 1965, p. 25.
38. Numbers in parentheses in the text refer to pages in *Left-Handed Liberty* (London, 1965).
39. "Questions of Expediency," p. 15.
40. V.S. Pritchett, "Bad King," *New Statesman* 69 (June 25, 1965): 1022.
41. "Who's for a Revolution?", p. 50.
42. Pritchett, "Bad King," p. 1022.

Chapter Six

1. *Soldier, Soldier, and Other Plays* (London, 1967), pp. 178, 179.
2. *The Royal Pardon* (London, 1967), p. 7; hereafter page references cited in parentheses in the text are to this edition.
3. "Interview: John Arden Talks to John Peter," *Sunday Times*, June 9, 1968, p. 53.
4. Ronald Bryden, "Romantic 'Muggins,'" *Observer*, June 16, 1968, p. 27.
5. "John Arden Talks to John Peter," p. 53.
6. D. A. N. Jones, "Muggins," *Listener* 79 (June 20, 1968): 817.
7. Bryden, "Romantic 'Muggins,'" p. 27.
8. Simon Trussler, "Postscript to Arden," *Observer*, June 16, 1968, p. 27. The serious conflicts between the Ardens and

CAST finally appear in print in Catherine Itzin's *Stages in the Revolution* (London, 1980), pp. 21–23, 342–44.

9. *The True History of Squire Jonathan and His Unfortunate Treasure* in *Two Autobiographical Plays* (London, 1971), p. 23; hereafter page references cited in parentheses in the text are to this edition.

10. See for example M[ichael] B[illington], "John Arden's High Spirits in New Play," *Times* (London), June 18, 1968, p. 12; Philip French, "Laughing Stocks," *New Statesman* 75 (June 28, 1968): 881; Michael Coveney, *"Squire Jonathan,"* *Financial Times*, June 28, 1973.

11. *Squire Jonathan*'s tantalizing difficulties are explored at length in my article with Virginia Evans, "Approaches to John Arden's *Squire Jonathan*," *Modern Drama* 13 (Feb., 1971): 360–65.

Chapter Seven

1. Quoted by Ira Peck, "Art, Politics and John Arden," *New York Times*, Apr. 10, 1966, Sec. 2, p. 3. "Half-and-Half Nelson" (anon.), *Observer*, Feb. 14, 1965, p. 23, outlined Arden's early plans.

2. *The Hero Rises Up* (London, 1969), p. 14; hereafter page references cited in parentheses in the text are to this edition.

3. Ronald Eyre, "Premature Death Certificate," *Listener* 80 (Nov. 21, 1968):695.

4. Ronald Bryden, "O'Casey and His Raw Torso," *Observer*, Sept. 14, 1969, p. 26.

5. The best of many biographies is probably *Nelson* by Carola Oman (London: Hodder & Stoughton, 1947). A play about Nelson by Terence Rattigan, *A Bequest to the Nation* (London: Hamish Hamilton, 1970), was staged in London two years later.

6. Ronald Bryden, "Emma, the Goddess from Merseyside," *Observer*, Color Magazine, Oct. 26, 1969, p. 75.

7. Albert Hunt, "Incongrous Heroics," *New Society* 12 (Nov. 14, 1968):727.

8. "Human Horatio," *Sunday Times*, Mar. 9, 1969, p. 57.

9. *The Bagman* in *Two Autobiographical Plays* (London, 1971), p. 37; hereafter page references cited in parentheses in the text are to this edition.

10. David Wade, "Radio Drama," *Plays and Players* 17 (Aug., 1970): 12; Peter Porter, "Arden's Dream," *New Statesman* 79 (Apr. 10, 1970): 525–26.

Chapter Eight

1. Anthony Thwaite, "ESP," *Listener* 88 (Nov. 30, 1972): 764.
2. *"The Island of the Mighty," Times* (London), Dec. 5, 1972, p. 17; Dec. 7, p. 19; Dec. 9. p. 15; Dec. 12, p. 17; Dec. 13, p. 15; Dec. 15, p. 15; Dec. 16, p. 13. "Distorted Meanings at the Aldwych," *Guardian*, Dec. 5, 1972, p. 12, and "Exit, Left Wing," Dec. 9, p. 10. Also John Arden, in collaboration with D'Arcy, "Playwrights on Picket," *To Present the Pretence*, pp. 159–72.
3. *The Island of the Mighty* (London, 1974), p. 38; hereafter page references cited in parentheses in the text are to this edition. The text was published earlier as centerfold insets in *Plays and Players*, 20 (Feb. and Mar., 1973). The numbering of scenes differs in the two texts, with minor changes in stage directions to make this possible, and the Notes are substantially different.
4. "David Jones Talks to *P & P*," *Plays and Players* 20 (Feb. 1973): 30; David Jones, "Writing on Sand," *Theatre 73*, ed. Sheridan Morley (London: Hutchinson, 1973), p. 66.
5. "The Matter of Britain," *Flourish*, no. 3, n.s. (1972–73), p. 1.
6. "David Jones Talks to *P & P*," p. 30.
7. "The Matter of Britain," p. 1.
8. "Production Notes," *Performance*, no. 7 (Fall, 1973), p. 141. This short passage is not reprinted in the Eyre Methuen text.
9. "David Jones Talks to *P & P*," p. 30.
10. John Peter, "Troubled Isle," *Times Educational Supplement*, Dec. 22, 1972, p. 30.
11. Harold Hobson, "This Other Eden," *Sunday Times*, Dec. 10, 1972, p. 36.
12. J. W. Lambert, "Plays in Performance," *Drama*, no. 108 (Spring, 1973), p. 18.
13. Frank Marcus, "Shades of Night," *Sunday Telegraph*, Dec. 10, 1972, p. 18; B. A. Young, *"The Island of the Mighty," Financial Times*, Dec. 7, 1972, p. 3.
14. Kenneth Pearson, "John Arden's TV Epic," *Sunday Times*, Feb. 16, 1969, p. 53.

Chapter Nine

1. Examples of Arden's discussions of Ireland are "John Arden-2," *Plays and Players* 19 (Dec., 1971): 14, and (with D'Arcy) "Censorship and Cultural Consensus," *The British Media and Ireland* (London: Campaign for Free Speech on Ireland, 1979), pp. 48–49.

2. "Radio Drama," *Plays and Players* 19 (Oct., 1971): 59.
3. "What's Theater For?," *Performance* 1 (Sept.–Oct. 1972):17, 11–12.
4. *Times* (London), Oct. 18, 1977, p. 2, and Dec. 2, 1977, p. 6.
5. D. J. Hart, "Home Premiere," *Times Educational Supplement*, Jan. 29, 1982, p. 27.
6. *The Little Gray Home in the West* (London, 1982), pp. 12–13; hereafter page references cited in parentheses in the text are to this edition.
7. *The Ballygombeen Bequest, Scripts*, no. 9 (Sept., 1972), p. 5.
8. Robert Brustein, "Two Plays about Ireland," *The Culture Watch* (New York: Knopf, 1975), pp. 55, 56.
9. Charles Lewsen, "Actors' Living Sculptures," *Times* (London), Aug. 29, 1972, p. 6.
10. Michael Anderson, "Edinburgh 72," *Plays and Players* 20 (Nov., 1972): 51.
11. Jonathan Hammond, "Fringe," *Plays and Players* 20 (Nov., 1972): 62; John Lahr, "Acting out the Protest," *New Statesman* 84 (Sept. 22, 1972): 408.
12. Brustein, "Two Plays about Ireland," p. 56.
13. "A Socialist Hero on the Stage," *To Present the Pretence*, pp. 100–1.
14. "Radio Drama," *Plays and Players*, p. 59.
15. Maria Kreisler, "Theatre of Argument," *Elizabethan Trust News* (Australia), no. 17 (Dec., 1975), p. 22; "A Socialist Hero on the Stage," pp. 103–4.
16. Quoted by Dave Robins, "Questions of History," *Plays and Players* 23 (Aug., 1976): 25.
17. "A Socialist Hero on the Stage," pp. 106–7, 98.
18. "Interstates Left," *Guardian*, May 22, 1976, p. 12.
19. *The Non-Stop Connolly Show* (London, 1977–78), p. 28; hereafter page references cited in parentheses in the text are to this edition. Parts 1 and 2 of the show are in a single volume; the other four parts are each in a separate volume.
20. Anon., "Theatre," *Time Out*, June 18–24, 1976.
21. Catherine Itzin, "Arden's Achievement 'Censored,'" *Tribune*, May 28, 1976, p. 7.
22. Harold Hobson, "The Heart of Darkness," *Sunday Times*, May 23, 1976, p. 37.
23. J[ohn] B[arber], "*The Non-Stop Connolly Cycle*," *Daily Telegraph*, May 18, 1976.
24. *Vandaleur's Folly* (London, 1981), p. 17; hereafter page references cited in parentheses in the text are to this edition.
25. Tony Allen and Mary Ann Lysaght, "*Vandaleur's Folly*,"

Plays and Players 26 (Feb., 1979): 33.

26. Jeremy Treglown, *"Vandaleur's Folly,"* *Times* (London), Nov. 15, 1978, p. 9.
27. Robin Thornber, *"Vandaleur's Folly,"* *Guardian*, Oct. 11, 1978, p. 10.
28. *Pearl* (London, 1979), p. 52; hereafter page references cited in parentheses in the text are to this edition.
29. Peter Porter, "Psychopomp," *New Statesman* 96 (July 7, 1978): 29.
30. Michael Billington, "Priceless *Pearl?*," *Radio Times*, July 15, 1978.
31. Michael Billington, *"Pearl* of Great Praise," *Guardian*, July 1, 1978, p. 11.
32. Billington, "Priceless *Pearl?*"
33. Ibid.
34. Porter, "Psychopomp," p. 29.
35. Billington, "Priceless *Pearl?*"
36. Quoted by Paul Vallely, "Spanish Shadows," *Radio Times*, Oct. 3, 1980, pp. 17, 19, 21.
37. Jeremy Brooks, "Playwright in the Vatican," *Sunday Times*, Oct. 5, 1980, p. 41.
38. Geoffrey Cannon, "Today's Choice," *Sunday Times*, July 5, 1981, p. 48.
39. Paul Vallely, "Blake's Lampoon," *Listener*, Oct. 16, 1980, p. 515; "Popish Plot," *Listener*, Oct. 9, 1980, p. 488.
40. Quoted by Paul Vallely, "Fiery Individualists," *Listener*, Feb. 18, 1982, p. 29.
41. Paula Neuss, "The Rector of Diss," *Times Literary Supplement,* Mar. 12, 1982, p. 281.

Chapter Ten

1. Jack Richardson, "Musgrave's Dance and Azdak's Circle," *Commentary* 41 (June 1966):75; D. A. N. Jones, *"Muggins,"* *Listener* 79 (June 20, 1968): 817.
2. Albert Hunt, *Arden: A Study of His Plays* (London, 1974), p. 143; Adrian Mitchell, "Priests and Prophets of the New Permissiveness," *The Permissive Society* (London: Panther, 1969), p. 38.
3. "Who's for a Revolution?" pp. 50–51.
4. Frank Cox, *"Left-Handed Liberty,"* *Plays and Players* 12 (Aug., 1965): 41.
5. This judgment appears to originate with Tom Milne in "A Touch of the Poet," *New Left Review*, no. 7 (Jan.–Feb., 1961),

and to be popularized by John Russell Taylor in *Anger and After* (London, rev. ed., 1969), pp. 83–85, and in his Introduction to *Three Plays* (Harmondsworth, 1964).
6. Cf. Simon Trussler, "Arden: An Introduction," *Encore*, no. 57 (Sept.–Oct., 1965), p. 5.
7. *To Present the Pretence*, p. 158.
8. Quoted by Paul Vallely, "John Arden's One-Man War against Authority," *Yorkshire Post*, Apr. 11, 1977, p. 6.

Selected Bibliography

PRIMARY SOURCES

1. Plays

Armstrong's Last Goodnight. London: Methuen, 1965; New
  York: Grove Press, 1967.

Ars Longa, Vita Brevis. Co-author Margaretta D'Arcy. *Encore*,
  no. 48 (Mar.–Apr. 1964), pp. 13–20. Reprinted in *Eight
  Plays for Schools* (London: Cassell, 1964).

The Ballygombeen Bequest. Co-author Margaretta D'Arcy.
  Scripts, no. 9 (Sept., 1972), pp. 4–50.

The Business of Good Government. Co-author Margaretta
  D'Arcy. London: Methuen, 1963; New York: Grove Press,
  1967.

The Hero Rises Up. Co-author Margaretta D'Arcy. London:
  Methuen, 1969.

Ironhand, adapted from Goethe's *Götz von Berlichingen*.
  London: Methuen, 1965.

The Island of the Mighty. Co-author Margaretta D'Arcy. London:
  Eyre Methuen, 1974. Also in *Performance*, no. 7 (Fall,
  1973), pp. 47–144.

Left-Handed Liberty. London: Methuen, 1965; New York: Grove
  Press, 1966.

The Little Gray Home in the West. Co-author Margaretta D'Arcy.
  London: Pluto, 1982. (Revised version of *The Ballygombeen
  Bequest*).

The Non-Stop Connolly Show. Co-author Margaretta D'Arcy.
  5 vols. London: Pluto, 1977–78.

Pearl. London: Eyre Methuen, 1979.

Plays One. London: Eyre Methuen, 1977. With a new Preface by
  Arden. Contains *Serjeant Musgrave's Dance, The Workhouse Donkey,* and *Armstrong's Last Goodnight*.

The Royal Pardon. Co-author Margaretta D'Arcy. London:
  Methuen, 1967.

Serjeant Musgrave's Dance. London: Methuen, 1960; New York:
  Grove Press, 1962. Methuen Student Edition, with commentary and notes by Glenda Leeming, 1982. Also in *The New*

British Drama, ed. Henry Popkin; New York: Grove Press, 1964.

Soldier, Soldier, and Other Plays. London: Methuen, 1967. Contains also *Wet Fish, When Is a Door Not a Door?,* and *Friday's Hiding* (co-author Margaretta D'Arcy).

Three Plays. Introduced by John Russell Taylor. Harmondsworth: Penguin, 1964; New York: Grove Press, 1966. Contains *The Waters of Babylon, Live Like Pigs,* and *The Happy Haven* (co-author Margaretta D'Arcy). *Live Like Pigs* previously published in *New English Dramatists, 3* (Harmondsworth: Penguin, 1961) and *The Happy Haven* in *New English Dramatists, 4* (Harmondsworth: Penguin, 1962).

Two Autobiographical Plays. London: Methuen, 1971. Contains *The True History of Squire Jonathan and His Unfortunate Treasure* and *The Bagman. The Bagman* reprinted in *Scripts,* no. 8 (Aug., 1972), pp. 85–110.

Vandaleur's Folly. Co-author Margaretta D'Arcy. London: Eyre Methuen, 1981.

The Workhouse Donkey. London: Methuen, 1964; New York: Grove Press, 1967.

2. Essays
To Present the Pretence. London: Eyre Methuen, 1977. Sixteen reprinted essays, 1964–77, an original lecture, and five new linking-pieces.

3. Selected articles and reviews
"Armstrong's Last Goodnight." Encore, no. 51 (Sept.–Oct., 1964), pp. 50–52.

"Brecht and the Brass Trade." *Guardian,* July 29, 1965, p. 6.

Children of Albion. Edited by Michael Horowitz. Harmondsworth: Penguin, 1969, pp. 14–20. (Four poems)

"Correspondence." *Encore,* no. 20 (May–June 1959), pp. 41–43. (On the nature of theater)

"Delusions of Grandeur." *Twentieth Century* 169 (Feb., 1961): 200–6.

"The Difficulty of Getting Things Done Properly." In *Effective Theatre,* edited by John Russell Brown, pp. 146–48. London: Methuen, 1969.

"Ecce Hobo Sapiens: O'Casey's Theatre." In *Sean O'Casey: A Collection of Critical Essays,* edited by Thomas Kilroy, pp. 61–76. Englewood Cliffs, N.J.: Prentice-Hall, 1975.

"The Fork in the Head." *Visitors Book,* pp. 33–44. Swords, Co. Dublin: Poolbeg, 1979. (His only short story)

"*Henry V,*" *New Statesman* 67 (June 19, 1964):946–47.

"How to Understand Hell." *Twentieth Century* 173 (Winter, 1964–65):99–101.

"Human Horatio." *Sunday Times*, Mar. 9, 1969, p. 57. (Review of *Nelson and the Hamiltons*, by Jack Russell)

"John Arden." In *All Bull*, edited by B.S. Johnson, pp. 230–42. London: Allison & Busby, 1973. (His army experiences)

"Poetry and Theatre." *Times Literary Supplement* (London), Aug. 6, 1964, p. 705.

"The Reps. and New Plays—A Writer's Viewpoint." *New Theatre Magazine* I (Jan., 1960):23–26.

"Rug-Headed Irish Kerns and British Poets." *New Statesman* 98 (July 13, 1979):56–57.

"Shakespeare: To a Young Dramatist." *Guardian*, Apr. 23, 1964, p. 11.

"Some Thoughts Upon Left-wing Drama." In *International Theatre Annual*, 5, edited by Harold Hobson, pp. 187–96, 201–3. London: John Calder, 1961.

"Telling a True Tale." In *The Encore Reader*, edited by Charles Marowitz, Tom Milne, and Owen Hale, pp. 125–29. London: Methuen, 1965.

"Theatre and Leisure." *Socialist Commentary*, Aug. 1964, pp. 29–31.

"Theatre for the Gods." *Peace News*, Oct. 25, 1963, p. 10.

"They Do But Jest." *New Statesman* 98 (Aug. 24, 1979):280–81.

"A Thoroughly Romantic View." *London Magazine* 7 (July, 1960):11–15.

"Verse in the Theatre." In *English Dramatic Theories*, edited by Paul Goetsch, pp. 111–18. Tubingen: Max Niemeyer Verlag, 1972. From *New Theatre Magazine* I (Apr., 1961): 12–17.

"What's Theatre For?" *Performance* I,4 (Sept.–Oct., 1972):9–18.

"Why Can't We See It?" *Sunday Times*, Nov. 12, 1961. (Review of *Curtmantle* by Christopher Fry)

4. Records and Tapes

The Poet Speaks. Vol. 6. London: Argo, 1965. Arden talks, and reads "Here I Come."

Here Today: Poems by 45 Contemporary Authors. Pt. 1. New Rochelle, N.Y.: Spoken Arts "Jupiter." "Johnny Finn" and "The Lobster Pot."

Twentieth Century Poets Reading Their Own Poetry. Twickenham, Middlesex: Audio-Visual Productions. "Johnny Finn," "The Lobster Pot," "Whose Dreams," "The Green Man," "Give Me a Mirror," and songs and speeches from five plays.

5. Selected Interviews

Arden, John. "Building the Play: an Interview," in *The New British Drama*, edited by Henry Popkin, pp. 581–606. New York: Grove Press, 1964. Reprinted from *Encore*, July–Aug., 1961. Partially reprinted in *Theatre at Work*, edited by Charles Marowitz and Simon Trussler, pp. 36–50. London: Methuen, 1967.

———. "Who's for a Revolution?: Two Interviews." *Tulane Drama Review*, no. 34 (Winter, 1966), pp. 41–53. The first interview, with Walter Wager, is reprinted in a fuller form in *The Playwrights Speak*, edited by Walter Wager, pp. 238–68. (New York: Dell, 1967). The second interview, with Simon Trussler, is reprinted in *Theatre at Work*, edited by Charles Marowitz and Simon Trussler, pp. 50–57 (London: Methuen, 1967), with minor additions.

———. "Writers and Television-2: The Writer's View; John Arden Interviewed by Alan Lovell." *Contrast* 2 (Winter, 1962): 124–33.

Hennessy, Brendan. "John Arden." *Transatlantic Review*, no. 40 (Summer, 1971), pp. 52–59.

Orr, Peter. *The Poet Speaks: Interviews with Contemporary Poets*, pp. 1–6. New York: Barnes & Noble, 1966.

"Playwriting for the Seventies." *Theatre Quarterly*, no. 24 (Winter, 1976–77), pp. 35–74. Symposium with Arden, D'Arcy, and 13 other playwrights.

SECONDARY SOURCES

1. Bibliographies

King, Kimball. *Twenty Modern British Playwrights: A Bibliography, 1956 to 1976*, pp. 1–26. New York: Garland, 1977.

Page, Malcolm. "Theatre Checklist No. 7: John Arden." *Theatrefacts*, no. 7 (1975), pp. 2–13.

Stoll, Karl-Heinz. *The New British Drama: A Bibliography with Particular Reference to Arden, Bond, Osborne, Pinter, Wesker*, pp. 9–10, 16–17, 24–27. Bern: Herbert Lang, 1975.

2. Books and Parts of Books

Anderson, Michael. *Anger and Detachment*, pp. 50–87. London:Pitman, 1976. Astute and admiring commentary.

Aylwin, A.M. *Notes on John Arden's "Serjeant Musgrave's Dance."* London: Methuen Educational "Study-Aid," 1976.

Bablet, Denis, and Jean Jacqout, eds. *Les Voies de la Crea-*

tion Théâtrale, 5, pp. 281–376. Paris: Centre de la Recherche Scientifique, 1977. French productions of *Armstrong* and *Live Like Pigs*.

Brown, John Russell. *Theatre Language*, pp. 190–234. London: Allen Lane Penguin Press, 1972. Studies various theater effects: patterns, pauses, gestures.

Browne, Terry W. *Playwrights' Theatre*. London: Pitman, 1975. History of the English Stage Company at the Royal Court Theater.

Elsom, John. *Post-War British Theatre*, pp. 98–100. London: Routledge & Kegan Paul, 1976.

————. *Post-War British Theatre Criticism*, pp. 167–74. London: Routledge & Kegan Paul, 1981. *Armstrong*.

Hayman, Ronald. *British Theatre since 1955: A Reassessment*. pp. 12–17. Oxford: Oxford University Press, 1979.

————. *The First Thrust*, pp. 79–82, 88–92. London: Davis-Poynter, 1975. *The Workhouse Donkey* and *Armstrong* at Chichester Festival.

————. *John Arden*. London: Heinemann Educational, 2d ed., 1969. Short study of the plays to *The Hero Rises Up*, with full plot summaries.

Hilton, Julian. "The Court and its Favours." In *Contemporary English Drama*, edited by C.W.E. Bigsby, pp. 147–155. London: Edward Arnold, Stratford-upon-Avon Studies, 19, 1981. Explores recurring Arden themes and characters.

Hinchliffe, Arnold P. *British Theatre 1950–1970*, pp. 76–88. Oxford: Blackwell, 1974.

Hunt, Albert. *Arden: A Study of His Plays*. London: Eyre Methuen, 1974. The only full-length account; essential but uneven.

Itzin, Catherine. *Stages in the Revolution*, pp. 21–38. London: Eyre Methuen, 1980. "Harold Muggins Is a Martyr" and afterwards.

Kennedy, Andrew. *Six Dramatists in Search of a Language*, pp. 213–29. Cambridge: Cambridge University Press, 1975. "Theatrical effectiveness" of the plays' language.

Lambert, J.W. *Drama in Britain 1964–1973*. London: Longmans for British Council, 1974.

Leeming, Glenda. *John Arden*. London: Longmans for British Council, 1974. Intelligent survey, in thirty pages.

Nightingale, Benedict. *An Introduction to Fifty Modern British Plays*, pp. 329–41. London: Pan, 1982. *Musgrave*.

Stone, Brian, and Clive Emsley. *"Venice Preserved," by Thomas Otway/"Serjeant Musgrave's Dance," by John*

Arden, pp. 23–34. Milton Keynes: Open University Press, 1976.

Taylor, John Russell. *Anger and After*, pp. 83–105. London: Methuen, rev. ed., 1969. As *The Angry Theatre* New York: Hill & Wang, 1969. The Arden section from the 1962 edition is reprinted in *Modern British Dramatists: A Collection of Critical Essays*, edited by John Russell Brown, pp. 83–97. (Englewood Cliffs, N.J.: Prentice-Hall, 1968). A balanced admirer outlines soundly the plays to 1965.

Trussler, Simon. *John Arden.* New York: Columbia University Press, 1973. Very good 48-page survey.

Tschudin, Marcus. *A Writer's Theatre: George Devine and the English Stage Company at the Royal Court, 1956–65*, pp. 99–132. Bern: Herbert Lang, 1972. *Musgrave* in performance, and its reviews.

Weiand, Hermann J. "John Arden." In *Insight IV: Analyses of Modern British and American Drama*, edited by Hermann J. Weiand, pp. 13–25. Frankfurt am Main: Hirschgraben-Verlag, 1976. *Musgrave.*

Worth, Katherine J. *Revolutions in Modern English Drama*, pp. 126–35. London: C. Bell, 1973. Arden's use of ballads and melodrama, and his involvement with audiences.

3. Articles

Blindheim, Joan Tindall. "John Arden's Use of the Stage." *Modern Drama* 11 (Dec., 1968): 306–16. Narrow chronological focus on this topic.

Corrigan, Robert W. "The Theatre of John Arden." *The Theatre in Search of a Fix*, pp. 316–24. New York: Delacorte Press, 1973. Deep, earnest analysis.

Day, Paul W. "Individual and Society in the Early Plays of John Arden." *Modern Drama* 18 (Sept., 1975): 239–49.

Dodd, P. "A Thematic Approach to John Arden's *Armstrong's Last Goodnight.*" *Revue des Langues Vivantes* 43 (1977): 323–29.

Epstein, Arthur D. "John Arden's Fun House." *University Review* 36 (June 1970): 243–51. *The Happy Haven.*

Gaskill, William. "Producing Arden." *Encore*, no. 57 (Sept.–Oct., 1965), pp. 20–26. Good; mainly on *Armstrong* from director's viewpoint.

Gilman, Richard. "Arden's Unsteady Ground." *Common and Uncommon Masks*, pp. 116–29. New York: Random House, 1971. Also in *Modern British Dramatists: A Collection of Critical Essays*, ed. John Russell Brown, pp. 104–16

(Englewood Cliffs, N.J.: Prentice-Hall, 1968). Difficult: plays in terms of spontaneous self versus abstractions.

Hampton, Nigel. "Freedom and Order in Arden's *Ironhand.*" *Modern Drama* 19 (June 1976): 129–33.

Klotz, Gunther. "Ein irisches Vermachtnis: *The Ballygombeen Bequest* von John Arden und Margaretta D'Arcy." *Zeitschrift fur Anglistik und Amerikanistik* 22 (1974): 419–24.

Lambert, J.W. "The Man in the Black-and-White Suit." *Times Literary Supplement*, (London) Mar. 3, 1978, p. 253. Considers what Arden has tried to do in 1970s.

Manchester, Victoria. "Let's Do Some More Undressing: The 'War Carnival' at New York University." *Educational Theatre Journal* 19 (Dec., 1967): 502–10. The Vietnam play.

Marsh, Paddy. "Easter at Liberty Hall." *Theatre Quarterly*, no. 20 (Dec., 1975–Feb., 1976), pp. 133–41. The first performance of *The Connolly Show*.

Messenger, Ann P. "John Arden's Essential Vision: Tragical-Historical-Political." *Quarterly Journal of Speech* 58 (1972): 307–12. The tragic conflict between inner and outer worlds, as in Krank, Musgrave, and Herod.

Mills, John. "Love and Anarchy in *Serjeant Musgrave's Dance.*" *Drama Survey* 7 (1968–69):45–51. Argument of the play is toward anarchy and away from all authority.

Milne, Tom. "The Hidden Face of Violence." In *Modern British Dramatists: A Collection of Critical Essays*, edited by John Russell Brown, pp. 38–46. Englewood Cliffs, N.J.: Prentice-Hall, 1968. *Musgrave*, Whiting's *Saint's Day*, and Pinter's *The Birthday Party*.

Page, Malcolm. "The Motives of Pacifists: John Arden's *Serjeant Musgrave's Dance.*" *Drama Survey* 6 (1967): 66–73.

———. "Some Sources of Arden's *Serjeant Musgrave's Dance.*" *Moderna Språk* 67 (1973): 332–41. Records differences between the prompt copy and published text; shows how Arden used various sources.

Page, Macolm, and Virginia Evans. "Approaches to John Arden's *Squire Jonathan.*" *Modern Drama* 13 (Feb., 1971): 360–65. Meaning of the play in the light of other Arden works: elements of ballads, politics, and inverted myth.

Rush, David. "Grief, but Good Order." *Moderna Språk* 58 (1964):452–58. Sound survey of *Musgrave*; admires the blend of "passion and control."

Shrapnel, Susan. "John Arden and the Public Stage." *Cam-*

bridge Quarterly 4 (Summer, 1969):225–36. Some Arden
plays seen in terms of their effort to communicate with the
audience.

Steinberg, M.W. "Violence in *Serjeant Musgrave's Dance*; A
Study in Tragic Antitheses." *Dalhousie Review* 57 (1977):
437–52.

Thorne, Barry. "*Serjeant Musgrave's Dance*: Form and Meaning," *Queen's Quarterly* 78 (Winter, 1971):567–71. Notes
"folk stylization" and the role of the Bargee.

Trussler, Simon. "Political Progress of a Paralyzed Liberal:
The Community Dramas of John Arden," *Drama Review*,
no. 44 (Summer, 1969), pp. 181–91. The first performances
of "Harold Muggins" and *The Hero Rises Up*.

Wardle, Irving. "Arden: Intellectual Marauder." *New Society*,
Dec. 9, 1965, pp. 22–23. Examines reasons for Arden's
relative failure to find audiences.

Index

169